This unique feminist handbook was written to help young
women reali...

men's roles are changing so rapidly. In particular, it is designed to encourage high school women to plan while they are still in school in order to realize the wide range of career and life styles that they can choose from. Nothing about a woman can be separated out of her life when she makes right decisions in education, religion, sex, friendship, sports, careers, arts, and leisure. The contributors to this invaluable book, all specialists in their field, show how good decision making can be achieved.

JOYCE SLAYTON MITCHELL was born in Hardwick, Vermont. She received an A.B. degree from Denison University and an M.S. degree from the University of Bridgeport. A consultant in education in Vermont, Ms. Mitchell is a former school counselor and author of many articles and books for helping high school students make good educational choices. She lives with her husband and two children in Wolcott, Vermont.

THE LAUREL-LEAF LIBRARY brings together under a single imprint outstanding works of fiction and nonfiction particularly suitable for young adult readers, both in and out of the classroom. The series is under the editorship of Charles F. Reasoner, Professor of Elementary Education, New York University, and Carolyn W. Carmichael, Associate Professor, Department of Communication Sciences, Kean College of New Jersey.

Other Choices for Becoming a Woman

revised edition

Joyce Slayton Mitchell

Published by
Dell Publishing Co., Inc.
1 Dag Hammarskjold Plaza
New York, New York 10017

Printed in the United States of America
First Laurel printing—September 1975

**To Elizabeth
with love . . .
and hope**

Contents

EDUCATIONAL CHOICES
In High School

Out of High School

CONTRIBUTORS

ROGER F. AUBREY, director of guidance and health education,
Brookline Public Schools, Massachusetts

DOUGLAS D. DILLENBECK, executive director of publications,
College Entrance Examination Board, New York City

MARY JANE GRAY, professor of obstetrics and gynecology,
University of Vermont College of Medicine

KENNETH B. HOYT, associate commissioner,
U.S. Office of Education, Washington, D.C.

BARBARA KRASNER, a family therapist, Eastern Pennsylvania
Psychiatric Institute, Philadelphia

DONNA LAWSON, author, reporter,
New York City

MARGARET MEAD, curator emeritus, The American Museum of
Natural History, New York City

JOYCE SLAYTON MITCHELL, consultant in education,
Wolcott, Vermont

NATALIE M. SHEPARD, professor emeritus,
Denison University, Ohio

JEAN STAPLETON, instructor of journalism,
East Los Angeles College, California

MONICA SCHLAG, pseudonym for a member of the Music
Department, Northern Illinois University

M. LYNETTE WARK, practicing physician,
Sydney, Australia

ACKNOWLEDGMENTS

It is with much admiration for the contributors that I thank each of them for their chapter. They represent a wide range of differences in their work and interests, but the diversity of the contributors is integrated by their role as teacher. Each is a very special teacher. My warmest thanks are extended to Roger Aubrey, Doug Dillenbeck, Mary Jane Gray, Ken Hoyt, Barbara Krasner, Donna Lawson, Margaret Mead, Natalie Shepard, Jean Stapleton, Monica Schlag, and Lyn Wark.

The curriculum chapter was read by Grace Butterweck, counselor, Irvington High School in New York, and Rocco Orlando, professor, Southern Connecticut State College in Connecticut. My thanks to both of them for their expertise in curriculum and counseling but especially for their time and interest in this book.

My appreciation goes to Aileen McGregor, New Zealand missionary in New Guinea, for teaching me about education through home study. Also to Pamela Hubbard who was my children's kindergarten and first-grade teacher in the New South Wales Correspondence School, Sydney, Australia.

I owe particular thanks to Shirley Matthews of Port Moresby, Papua, New Guinea, for her communications to me from the outer world to the inner New Guinea bush with materials for this book.

I am indebted to the Reverend Patricia Budd Kepler, Harvard Divinity School, for permission to quote from her speech given at the 1973 General Assembly of the United Presbyterian Church USA. More than that, I thank Pat for our work together on the concept of the spiritual equality for girls and women in our task force on Women and Religion in the National Organization for Women (NOW).

It's a pleasure to thank Lois Wark for her contribution to the Christian chapter.

I will be forever grateful to everyone at KNOW, Inc., whose interest in this project and rearrangement of their publishing schedule first got this book into print.

I want to thank Barbara Francis and Ron Buehl for their creative and caring editorial suggestions.

To Parker B. Ladd I always wish to express my thanks for his friendship, his encouragement, and his affirmation of my work before it even begins until after it's finished.

And thanks with love to Bill, Ned, and Elizabeth who are in on everything—this book too.

JSM
Wolcott, Vermont

FOREWORD

That a book like this is necessary, and it is, may be a commentary on the sexism in our society and its social institutions, including education. The contributions herein should help put sex in its place; girls and women need not accept any restrictions. We all need to explore our full human potential to include our sexuality, and our spiritual, intellectual, and social development. While addressed to girls, I would suggest this book lends itself to a "read-in" by parents and other educators, by boys and men who care about girls and women.

Indeed, caring is central to what Joyce Slayton Mitchell is about. It's about time caring women and men help girls and women toward the direction that leads to self-discovery. The rebirth of feminism means that girls have transcended their sexual role to find and love themselves and others, exploring every dimension of human experience, uninhibited by sex-role stereotyping and denial of self and their worth.

It is the end of real or feigned innocence for girls and women. The masks of play acting are off, this drama is for real! I would consider this book to be a public health and public education measure. Sexism is a social disease; feminism-humanism is the cure. Were I the presiding physician, one of the treatments I would prescribe would be: Rx, Other Choices for Becoming a Woman.

WILMA SCOTT HEIDE, *Past President,*
National Organization for Women (NOW)

Who Chooses?

A Person Chooses

JOYCE SLAYTON MITCHELL

Many teachers, counselors, and parents act as if they know who you will be and what you should choose. You should take foreign languages instead of mathematics; you should study the social sciences rather than the physical sciences; and you should decide to be a teacher, nurse, or secretary until you get married or in case something happens to your husband. Of course, they say, if these things don't fit, it isn't too serious because you will choose marriage rather than a career anyway. Most educators assume that your decision to get married will take the place of a serious career commitment as if there were only one choice—marriage or career—rather than the multi-life styles of American women today. They assume that you are going to choose the role of wife/mother rather than be a person who can choose to be anything.

When you begin to see yourself developing as a whole person with many choices rather than a half marriage partner with no choice, you will work through your own values to develop a life style of your own. You will begin to rely more on your own experiences and feelings of self-discovery—and less on the cultural expectations for girls.

Other Choices is designed as a catalyst, a beginning for learning more about you. You have to discover all the things you are and can be before you can know how to choose. A person discovers what she is like and then decides what she will do about it. This book will help you to decide.

Good decisions are made when you have yourself altogether, an integrated person. There isn't anything about you that can be separated out of your life as if it isn't related to your decisions. Your sexuality, schoolwork, and all your friendships, your spirituality and your summer time—all count as you are learning to realize your potential as a woman and are planning for *Other Choices*.

MORE INFORMATION FOR BECOMING A WOMAN

There are thousands of feminist publications for every interest of every girl and woman. The following addresses are a place to begin to look for more information. Remember, a feminist is a person (male or female) who believes in the possibility and the right for a female to have equality in *all* choices. And those choices are *yours!*

NATIONAL ORGANIZATION FOR WOMEN (NOW). The largest feminist organization with over 600 chapters, which work in 27 task-force areas of concern to bring equality to women.
Write to: NOW, 5 South Wabash Avenue, Suite 1615, Chicago, IL 60603.
Ask for: The NOW chapter nearest you and/or specific information about their activities that interest you.

KNOW, INC. A nonprofit feminist press that publishes reprints of feminist articles, a series of female studies, a list of recently published feminist books (10 cents), and a list of feminist periodicals and publications (15 cents).

Write to: KNOW, Inc., P.O. Box 86031, Pittsburgh, PA 15221.

Ask for: Their publication list or any of the lists mentioned above.

Ms. MAGAZINE. The first and only feminist magazine on the newsstand. Look in your local library for *Ms.*, July 1973 issue, for the excellent descriptions of over 65 feminist magazines, newspapers, and newsletters. You will find them on pages 95–98.

To subscribe, write: Ms., 123 Garden Street, Marion, OH 43302. $9 per year.

WOMEN'S HISTORY RESEARCH CENTER. A library collection with over 5,000 feminist publications and half of them are available on microfilm. For information and a brochure write: Women's History Research Center, 2325 Oak Street, Berkeley, CA 94708

Sexual Choices

Learning about Sex

MARY JANE GRAY

Mary Jane Gray, M.D., is a physician who lectures about sex education, a marriage counselor, and a consultant for a women's health center. Most important, she is concerned about you and your understanding of sex.

Dr. Gray, professor of obstetrics and gynecology at the University of Vermont College of Medicine, details the specific facts about physical maturity, intercourse, pregnancy, contraception, abortion, homosexuality, and venereal disease. She encourages you to understand that moral behavior (being honest with yourself and others) toward your friends and family leads to a self-understanding that should be the basis for your sexual decisions.

Just when you are beginning to feel the social and biological pressures directing you closer toward femaleness, you are likely to encounter the greatest difficulty in finding the answers to questions about sex. Your friends and contemporaries may be approachable, but many of their "facts" are wrong; and their range of experience is little greater than your own.

Parents should be available as a source of help, but many, perhaps remembering the discomfort of their own youth and doubting the adequacy of their knowledge in this area, back away. They may not wish to probe their children in such a personal matter, or they may forget the urgency of the questions, or they may wish to protect your "innocence."

This chapter will help you understand you.

A REVIEW OF SPECIFICS

Each woman's body proceeds on its course toward maturity at its own rate, controlled by the genes with which it is endowed. Serious illness or marked malnutrition may vary this slightly, but all the wishing in the world will not make the short, tall; the fair, dark; or the large-boned, dainty. Learning to accept the realities of one's own body is a difficult part of growing up. These same considerations extend to the sexual organs as well. Pubic hair will grow, breasts will bud, menstruation will start, and genitalia will reach adult form on a predetermined schedule whether one is impatient for these external signs of physical maturity or whether one would prefer to wait. In the end practically everyone emerges with the physical equipment capable of all that the adult will ask of it. Differences in age of maturing and size and shape of breasts turn out to be as unimportant as the color of one's eyes. Yet, accepting these changes and the sexual feelings that come with them is difficult for most young people. The next few pages review briefly normal physiology and anatomy.

Puberty in the Female

The first sign of beginning sexual maturity in the girl is usually the growth of hair in the armpits and in the pubic area, caused in part by hormones from the adrenal glands. Shortly thereafter, estrogen, the chief female hormone, starts the breasts to grow, first with a tender fullness under the nipples and then, over several years, to develop the classic feminine contour. Movies and TV have projected such a false image of the size and function of the female breast that many young people do not realize that its biological function, producing milk, is totally unrelated to size. It is very common for one breast to be a little larger than the other, especially in the early stages of development. Meanwhile, growth and development of the external genital organs, or vulva, is taking place. The more sensitive labia minora, or inner lips, are formed of a moist mucous membrane.

While these external changes are taking place, the internal sexual organs—the vagina, uterus (womb), tubes, and ovaries—are beginning to grow. The ovaries produce the estrogens which cause maturation of these organs as well as contain the developing eggs or ova. With continued hormonal stimulation, the endometrium, or lining of the uterus, becomes thicker and suitable for an egg to implant if one is fertilized. If pregnancy does not occur, the level of estrogen temporarily drops, the lining of the uterus breaks down, and blood appears at the opening of the vagina, the beginning of the first menstrual period. Thereafter, a cyclic pattern is set up. It is customary to number the days in this cycle starting with the first day of bleeding, or menstruation. Approximately 12 to 16 days after the beginning of a menstrual period, an egg is released by the ovary. This is picked up by the end of the fallopian tube which carries the egg to the uterus. If pregnancy does not occur, the egg disintegrates, estrogen levels drop, and another menstrual period begins, approximately 26 to 32 days after the last.

The great variation in length, duration, and interval of normal periods is not generally understood. At the beginning, while the pattern is being established, irregularity of interval and length of flow is frequent. Later, most girls develop a pattern that is their own, and they learn to recognize variation from this. Bleeding should rarely last over a week, and any flow not easily controlled by the usual sanitary napkins or tampons should be brought to a doctor's attention.

Many myths about menstrual periods flourish. Periods are not an illness; they are the outward sign of normal function. Exercise, including swimming, is to be encouraged, and baths and showers are a must. Wash your hair! Occasional mild cramps and other minor discomforts may occur. If a couple of aspirin tablets and the normal distractions of your daily life are not enough to keep you in circulation, see your doctor.

Somewhat more variably, but normally, sexual feelings and urges arise in the female. The clitoris, which is the feminine structure somewhat like the penis, is the area that is most sensitive. In many girls, sexual tensions are released by masturbation (stimulation of the genitals). Despite lingering tales of earlier generations, this does not cause any physical or mental harm and can be an aid in normal sexual development.

Other changes at puberty include a tendency to acne which relates to a change in hormone balance, and increasing perspiration, especially under the arms.

Puberty in the Male

In the boy, hormonal changes cause the growth of hair under the arms and in the pubic area around the penis, a sign of beginning sexual maturation. This is followed by growth of the penis itself, the testes, and the covering skin of the scrotum as well as spurts of general body growth. Changes in the shape of the larynx or voice box cause a deepening of the voice. Gradually, coarse hair grows on other parts of the body including the beard. Sweat and oil glands mature, leading to increased perspiration odors as well as a tendency toward acne.

Meanwhile, changes are taking place with the testes or male sex glands themselves. The cells have begun to produce testosterone, the chief male hormone, which in turn causes most of the other characteristics of the adult male. Cells called spermatocytes begin to mature into sperm cells capable of independent movement and of fertilizing eggs. Other ducts and glands in the male reproductive tract begin to secrete seminal fluid suitable for carrying the sperm toward their destination and nourishing them on their long journey. Sperm are stored in a reservior known as the seminal vesicle and from there are ejaculated with the seminal fluid as semen. Each ejaculation contains about 200 million sperm. Even though the male uses the same ducts to pass urine and to ejaculate sperm, the valves or controls are such that it is impossible for both processes to happen at once. Urine is never part of the semen.

From birth to death the penis is capable of becoming firm and erect in response to many sorts of stimulation. Venous channels fill with blood and increase the size and consistency of the penis. Only after puberty does sexual stimulation cause the ejaculation of fluid from the erect penis. At this point the boy is physically capable of fathering a child. The penis responds with erection to many sorts of stimuli in addition to the specifically sexual and is not altogether under the conscious control of the young man. Ejaculation, however, occurs only after sexual arousal, including that taking place in dreams. Such dreams, called "wet dreams" or nocturnal emissions, are completely normal. Sexual tensions are also frequently released by manual stimulation of the genitals to climax (orgasm, ejaculation). This is called masturbation, and is almost universal in adolescent boys.

Intercourse

When the erect penis is placed in the female vagina, and stimulated so that ejaculation occurs, the act is called sexual intercourse, or coitus. The vagina produces lubrication during preliminary stimulation which makes entry of the penis easy. The hymen is a partial membrane around the vaginal opening which is easily stretched by tampons and foreplay and rarely a true

barrier. The positions used for intercourse are determined by the inventiveness and pleasure of the individuals involved and have no particular significance.

The female sexual response, or orgasm, consists of
vaginal contractions as well as general body reactions
such as rapid pulse and breathing. Recent studies have
shown that there are many similarities between male
and female sexual response, even though the actual sex
organs differ. Much has been made of the woman's
ability to respond repeatedly. She tends to be very
sensitive to the circumstances in which intercourse
takes place, and the quality of the total experience is
more important to her than the number of orgasms.
Not all women respond during their early sexual experiences; they may require time to develop confidence,
trust, and relaxation necessary to make sex a good
experience.

Pregnancy

If any one of the hundreds of millions of sperm
reaches the fallopian tube in the female just at the time
that an egg is ready to be fertilized, they may unite,
and a pregnancy begins. This is usually midway between menstrual periods, but varies widely. The tiny
sperm are capable of motion by means of a tadpole-
like tail and can occasionally travel far enough to fer-
tilize an egg even if deposited just outside the entrance
to the vagina. The sperm move very rapidly and washing out the vagina (douching) will not prevent pregnancy.

The fertilized egg moves down the tube into the
uterus and embeds itself in the lining, or endometrium,
about ten days later. The developing embryo sends a
hormonal message back to the ovary so that estrogen
continues to be made in increasing quantities and menstruation does not take place. Thus the skipping of a
period may be a sign of pregnancy, but there are other
causes of missed periods, especially in the early teens.
A second female hormone, progesterone, is also pro-

duced in large quantities during pregnancy; together with estrogen, it is capable of producing the changes in the body necessary for the successful carrying of a baby for the usual nine months required for full development.

The date of delivery is about 280 days after the last menstrual period. At that time labor begins with regular contractions of the muscles in the wall of the uterus, a little like menstrual cramps. With these contractions, the cervix or mouth of the uterus gradually opens and the baby's head moves into the vagina. The vagina can stretch enough for the baby to pass through. Frequently, however, a small cut is made at the opening of the vagina so that the baby's head can slip out more easily. This is sewed up immediately afterward. About five minutes after the baby is born, the placenta, or afterbirth, is expelled. This platelike structure attaches the baby to the mother's uterus by means of the umbilical cord and is the place where oxygen, carbon dioxide, nutrients, and wastes are exchanged.

Prevention of Pregnancy

No one should consider sexual intercourse without deciding *in advance* whether or not a resulting pregnancy is desirable. About 80 percent of normal women having intercourse regularly will become pregnant in one year if steps are not taken to prevent this.

In discussing contraception, or birth control, you must consider which methods are the most reliable (will almost always prevent pregnancy), which methods are the safest for the people using them, and which methods are available. There is not yet any method which is 100 percent reliable and 100 percent safe, but there are some very good ones.

The most reliable methods now available are the *pill* (almost 100 percent effective) and the *IUD* or intrauterine device (95–98 percent effective). Contraceptive pills are a combination of the two types of female hormones, estrogen and progesterone. They must be

taken daily by mouth for three out of four weeks each
month. The body responds as if ovulation (release of
an egg) had already taken place, therefore preventing
ovulation from occurring. Although there are some rare
complications associated with the use of "the pill,"
these occur less frequently than do pregnancy complications. The IUD is made of flexible plastic in a shape
which can be introduced into the cavity inside the
uterus through the cervix. The method is easier for
women who have been pregnant, but is used successfully by many who have not.

Both these methods require consultation with a doctor. An increasing number of physicians realize that
the physical and emotional risks of unwanted pregnancy are high and therefore are willing to discuss the
problems of the young and unmarried. The *vaginal dia-
phragm,* which imposes a rubber and chemical barrier
to sperm, also needs to be fitted by a doctor. This
method is fairly good if used regularly (80–95 percent
effective) but requires careful advanced planning.

The *condom* is a rubber sheath which fits over the
erect penis and acts as a barrier, preventing the sperm
from entering the vagina. It is about 90 percent reliable, but the effectiveness can be improved by the
woman using vaginal contraceptive foam at the same
time. They are both available in drugstores without
prescription. Foam alone is not a good preventive (70
percent effective).

Most of the other methods should be mentioned only
to say that they do not work well. *Rhythm* is particularly unreliable to the teen-ager, whose periods may
vary. Pregnancies have been documented on every day
of the menstrual cycle, and even with those whose
periods are very regular, there are frequent failures.
Douching (washing out the vagina) should be mentioned only to condemn it since the sperm start at the
cervix and travel out of reach in seconds. Makeshift
plastic condoms are not at all as safe as the commercial rubber ones. *Withdrawal* (pulling the penis out
before ejaculation) requires more control than most

young men possess and frequently leaves the woman unsatisfied.

Abortion

When a fetus is expelled before the twentieth week of pregnancy, the process is called abortion. The artificial removal of the pregnancy from the uterus is called an *induced* abortion. Some pregnancies end naturally at two or three months because the embryo is not developing as it should. This is called a miscarriage, or more properly, a *spontaneous* abortion.

If people always used the best methods of contraception, induced abortions would rarely be necessary. They are inconvenient and involve some risks and some physical and mental discomfort. There has been a recent change in attitude toward abortion, however, as the hazards of premature marriage and unwanted children have become more apparent. The 1973 Supreme Court decision has made abortion legal throughout the United States, although some states have been slow in accepting this change.

If you think you may be pregnant, tell your parents as soon as possible. They may not be happy about it, but most parents behave better than you would think in this situation and they may be able to help you solve your problems. If you cannot face your parents alone, enlist the help of some responsible adult. If the solution is to be abortion, the sooner it is done, the safer. Counseling services are available through Planned Parenthood and other agencies in most parts of the country.

Abortion is not the only or necessarily the best answer to the unwanted pregnancy. It is frequently possible to have the baby adopted into a home where it will receive good care by two mature parents. Marriage is seldom a good idea for teen-agers when a pregnancy has occurred. The divorce rate under these conditions is about 75 percent. Trying to have a baby and keep it when one is young and unmarried is difficult since the support and care of the child must rest with the girl's parents if she is untrained to support herself. In addition, unfair though it is, our society makes difficulties for the child born under these circumstances.

Masturbation

The physical release of tension following sexual stimulation is called a climax, or orgasm, regardless of whether this occurs as the result of self-stimulation, petting, or intercourse. Masturbation, sometimes referred to in the male as "jerking off," is the act of stimulation of one's own genitals. Many myths deep in our culture tell us that such activity will result in acne, insanity, or damage to the sex organs. This is nonsense! The only adverse effects of masturbation are guilt feelings in those who have been raised to consider this act wrong and a momentary decrease in the drive for sexual activity in other directions. Only if one never advanced beyond masturbation as a sexual outlet, or if one masturbated so frequently that it interfered with other activities, could it have a bad effect. The vast majority of people of both sexes occasionally masturbate. It's a natural part of your sexual development.

Homosexuality

Most children have friends chiefly of their own sex. In the early teens sexual experimentation between members of the same sex sometimes occurs. This is usually a passing stage of development. In the usual course of growing up, friendships with the same sex are supplemented by those involving the opposite sex which begin to arouse feelings leading to increasing involvement as the relationship grows. When people turn to others of their own sex as their preferred partners in a sexual relationship, they are termed homosexuals and in slang terminology are sometimes called "gay." Women homosexuals are known as lesbians. In our society there are strong stereotypes of what constitutes masculine and feminine behavior. The term homosexual is sometimes misapplied to people who do not conform to society's stereotype of what a woman (or man) should look like or act like. Although formerly considered to be psychologically abnormal, most psychiatrists now think that homosexuals are like others except in the area of sex preference.

It may be reassuring to know that many women and men have had homosexual relationships in early adolescence and later established sexual relationships with individuals of the opposite sex. In addition, some people seem to function in either homosexual or heterosexual relationships and may be termed *bisexual*. There remain, nonetheless, many legal and strongly disapproving restrictions against homosexual behavior in our society which means that any homosexual activity tends to arouse anxiety.

Problems frequently arise because most of the world does not understand homosexuality and therefore is very intolerant of this kind of activity. If you are concerned about the possibility that you may be inclined to prefer a sexual relationship with another young woman, find a trusted friend to discuss the matter with you. You can also look for further information in such books as Pomeroy's *Girls and Sex* and *Our Bodies, Ourselves*.

Venereal Disease

A few diseases are passed from one person to another almost entirely by sexual intercourse and have been designated as the venereal diseases. The organisms that cause them are well known, cures are readily available, and the association with sex is the only excuse for the aura of mystery that still prevails. The two common venereal diseases are syphilis and gonorrhea.

Syphilis is caused by a microorganism called a spirochete which is easily killed by drying and must be passed from one moist mucous membrane to another immediately. The period between exposure and development of symptoms is usually two to three weeks, and the primary form of the disease appears first as a sore on the genitals. This is more easily noticed on the penis than in the vagina. The primary sore may heal without treatment, but the infection reaches the bloodstream and eventually many organs of the body including the heart and brain. The disease may be diagnosed by examination of the primary sore or, later, by a blood test. A course of penicillin treatments will cure the disease in any stage.

Much more common and now epidemic among sexually active youths is gonorrhea, commonly known as G.C., or "the clap." This is caused by a bacterium, the gonococcus, which, like the spirochete, is very fragile and dies quickly without a warm, moist place to grow. After an incubation period of two to six days, a discharge of pus appears from the penis in the male or the vagina in the female. Frequent urination with burning is common to both. In later stages, the infection may spread to other parts of the reproductive tract, eventually causing sterility if untreated, but it usually does not spread to distant parts of the body. This disease is also cured by penicillin and by several other antibiotics.

Only a doctor can diagnose venereal disease and institute the necessary treatment. Go for help immediately if you suspect that you may be infected. There are other conditions that may cause the same symptoms as venereal disease, so don't jump to conclusions. If you do have such an infection, however, be sure to tell your sexual partner so he can also be treated.

EMOTION, LOVE, AND SEX

One of the major tasks of the teen years is to acknowledge sexual feelings and impulses and to accept and control these, just as at a younger age you learned to accept and control anger and bring it under rational control. Friendships develop and the recognition of the contribution of sex to love is not always easy. Yet both attraction and love are part of happy, supportive relationships.

The development of independence from parents in preparation for the eventual leaving home takes place at the same time, and sometimes the tasks of adolescence get confused. The need to learn to make decisions on your own does not mean that the decision itself must be radically different from the one your parents would advise. The important thing is to figure out what you are for, not what you are against. The pressure for conformity to the standards of your friends may be even stronger than that of your parents. In the end, however, genuine independence means being able to take care of yourself in a way that meets with *your own* approval and permits you to make a place in the world and contribute to the welfare of others.

This may not be a time of sexual revolution, but it is a time in which sexual standards and customs are changing and reasonable people differ about what is right. A brief discussion of some of the standards that coexist in our society may help you sort out conflicting views. The traditional Judeo-Christian ethic has held that *premarital chasity* is the only proper mode of behavior, followed by fidelity after marriage. When this standard is broken by one who holds it, the guilt that results may cause major problems.

The double standard, which permits all sorts of sexual activity on the part of the male but insists on virginity in the female, is hard to defend but is still widespread. It is far more popular with men than with women and more popular in south than in north. It is used as an excuse by exploitive males to sleep with a girl, then depart. Fortunately, the honesty of the younger generation is reducing the hold of the double standard.

Permissiveness with affection is the term applied to the standard that says that anything is proper between people who love each other. The practical problems that can arise from this are many, especially when those involved are young, but the underlying assumptions of mutual agreement and love are popular. Most extreme is *general permissiveness,* which equates sex with recreation and says that, between consenting adults, anything goes.. Attractive as this may seem at first glance, this code is frequently used as an excuse for an inability to form close relationships and is generally not compatible with the quality of sex that is basic to a good marriage.

Perhaps more meaningful than the term premarital sex is *premature* sex. For almost all people, sexual attraction is one of the ingredients that leads them toward marriage. Sexual involvement tends to be slowly but surely progressive, reinforcing the emotional interaction in a good relationship. Studies have shown that intercourse, if engaged in early in a relationship, often speeds the breakup of the pair because it produces interpersonal stresses greater than the immature can handle. The farther you go sexually, the more it will hurt if you break up. The love, trust, privacy, and commitment required for good sex do not come easily to the young outside marriage.

But even marriages may be premature! Among the risks of premature commitment are those of curtailed education and reduced life goals. Compromises made in youth may be resented by the unfulfilled in middle age. The risk of divorce is 50 percent when two teenagers marry, and 75 percent if the girl is already pregnant. Intercourse introduces the woman to a new level of physical risks involving pregnancy or contraception as well as increased emotional risks. She should be sure that she understands and accepts these freely before taking this step. The responsible male must be willing to assume these risks with her.

Don't fall into the habit of thinking about virginity as a disease to be overcome. Intercourse can be one of the greatest or one of the loneliest, most hurtful experiences a woman can experience. Wait until you are ready for it and have a partner genuinely concerned about you, or you may find you have set up reactions that interfere with good sex in the future.

Although this chapter may seem to consider sex as something to be discussed, considered, and decided in a different way from other problems in life, this is not the intent. The same concepts of concern for the welfare of others and adherence to your own values and those of your family apply. Table 1 may help you in sorting out some general principles which apply to *all* relationships and which can be helpful regardless of your ethical background. If you do not value yourself, you have nothing to give to others.

Table I. Moral and Immoral Behavior

Moral Behavior Leads to	Immoral Behavior Leads to
Integrity in relationships	Duplicity in relationships
Trust in others	Distrust in others
Broadening of human sympathies	Barriers between persons and between groups
Cooperative attitudes	Uncooperative, hostile attitudes
Enhanced self-respect	Diminished self-respect
Consideration for rights and needs of others	Exploitation of others
Individual fulfillment and zest for living	Stunting of individual growth; disillusionment

Source: From *Sex and Our Society* by Lester A. Kirkendall, Public Affairs Pamphlet No. 366, Public Affairs Committee, Inc.

The fundamental task, then, for the teen-age girl is to get to know people of both sexes, coming to appreciate the differences in viewpoint of the sexes as well as the underlying human similarity. Value your friends for themselves and not as "dates" or "security" or for some other selfish or immature goal. Come to terms with your own sexuality, recognizing it as a valuable part of yourself, neither to be rejected nor exploited out of context. All this will take time.

In establishing your plans, think about your relationships in the cold light of morning. The notion of being swept off one's feet has romantic appeal, but it is a very immature way to deal with situations that may affect the rest of your life. And if you don't know your partner well enough to discuss your doubts, hopes, and fears regarding sex, you certainly don't know that person well enough to be contemplating an increased level of sexual activity. The earlier you become deeply involved, the more likely you are to marry early and take on adult responsibilities without the education and maturity necessary for success. Concern for the welfare and happiness of the other is the distinguishing characteristic of love.

FURTHER READINGS ABOUT SEX

From the hundreds of books written about sex for teens, Dr. Gray recommends the following list. If your high school library does not have them, try your public library or the nearest college library.

AMERICAN FRIENDS SERVICE COMMITTEE. *Who Shall Live? Man's Control Over Birth and Death.* New York: Hill & Wang, 1970. A thoughtful consideration of the ethical problems of contraception, abortion and death.

BLUFORD, ROBERT, AND PETRES, ROBERT. *Unwanted Pregnancy: The Medical and Ethical Considerations.* New York: Harper & Row, 1973. A clergyman and a doctor consider the problems surrounding unwanted pregnancy from a viewpoint that favors abortion.

BOSTON WOMEN'S HEALTH COLLECTIVE. *Our Bodies, Ourselves.* New York: Simon & Schuster, 1973. A book of information and feelings about women's bodies by women.

COX, F. D. *Youth, Marriage and the Seductive Society.* Dubuque, Iowa: William C. Brown Co., 1974. Influences of advertising, television, and other media in modern society on our view of sex and marriage.

CRAWLEY, L. Q., ET AL. *Reproduction, Sex and Preparation for Marriage.* Englewood Cliffs, New Jersey: Prentice-Hall, 1964. A good fundamental textbook consideration of the issues in the title.

DEMAREST, R. J. AND SCIARRA, J. J. *Conception, Birth and Contraception.* New York: McGraw-Hill, 1969. Best illustrations available.

GUTTMACHER, ALAN F. *Understanding Sex: A Young Person's Guide.* New York: New American Library, 1970. A straightforward consideration of the reproductive organs, sex, pregnancy, and contraception. No illustrations.

HETTLINGER, R. F. *Living with Sex: The Student's Dilemma.* New York: Seabury Press, 1966. A thoughtful consideration of the problems faced by young people coming to terms with their own sexuality.

Interview with Sex. Summerville, N.J.: Educational Services, 1970. An imaginary dialogue between love and sex, underlining some of the basic problems differentiating between the two.

JOHNSON, E. AND JOHNSON, C. *Love and Sex and Growing Up.* Philadelphia: Lippincott, 1970. A good discussion of these problems for the younger high school student.

KIRKENDALL, L. A. *Premarital Intercourse and Interpersonal Relationships.* New York: Julian Press, 1961. A classical study of what happens to relationships of varying degrees of commitment once intercourse is undertaken.

LIBERMAN, E. J., AND PECK, E. *Sex and Birth Control: A Guide for the Young.* New York: Thomas Crowell, 1973. An up-to-date and detailed book discussing contraception and sexual behavior in a practical straightforward manner.

NEWBARDT, S. *Contraception.* New York: Simon & Schuster, 1967. The pros and cons of the different methods of contraception by an author with a sense of humor. Slightly old, the contents have not changed.

PIERCE, R. *Single and Pregnant.* Boston: Beacon Press, 1970. A presentation of the various alternatives the high school girl faces if she finds that she is pregnant.

POMEROY, W. B. *Girls and Sex.* New York: Delacorte Press, 1966. A straightforward account of female sexuality from a liberal viewpoint.

RUBIN, I. AND KIRKENDALL, L. *Sex in the Adolescent Years.* New York: Association Press, 1968. A multi-authored consideration of various problems confronting the adolescent in dealing with sex.

SALTMAN, J., ED. *Sex, Love and Marriage.* New York: Grosset & Dunlap, 1968. Standard problems relating to sex and marriage by many authors.

SCHOFIELD, M. *The Sexual Behavior of Young People.* Boston: Little, Brown, 1965. A study of what was actually happening among young people in England in the early 1960s.

Deciding about Sex

JOYCE SLAYTON MITCHELL

Technological advances in the prevention of pregnancy do not give sexual freedom to girls. Sexual freedom comes only when you can decide for yourself—because you are a sexual being—what you are going to do sexually.

If you are of childbearing age, you can't really be serious about your life plans, college placement, or career unless you deal directly with your sexuality. You have to make unique decisions. Unique because you, and only you, actually carry and have a baby. All the compromises and sharing and taking turns of rearing a child cannot in any way be shared before the actual birth. Moreover, the discrimination against pregnancy, which is well illustrated in the world of work, cannot be shared. Advancement problems of young women in their careers, and negative attitudes of business and government toward maternity leave, are everywhere.

Our school system is notorious for ignoring your sexuality. Yet, it cannot be separated out of your life from your educational and career planning and decision making.

Everyone knows that today's high school girl has much less fear of pregnancy since the pill and the easier access to abortion. But what everyone does not know is that few people are trying to think about reasons other than the fear of pregnancy to cope with the sexual life styles of today that say it is easier to take the pill than to say no. That say something is wrong with you if you're seventeen and still a virgin. That don't say, Will you? but, How good will you be? That say sharing a bed is easier than sharing an evening. The pill often means more pressure for you to do what the boys want to do and, according to Karen DeCrow, author of *The Young Woman's Guide to Liberation,* "Virginity is no longer what the boys want (most of them); athletic and participating bed partners is what they want. So, girls go to bed before marriage *because boys want it that way.*"

Many adults who are in professions that are supposed to be helping adolescent girls have the misconception that today, because you have the pill, you have a new sexual freedom. New ways to prevent pregnancy do NOT give you sexual freedom! As long as you are doing sexually what the boys want—whether that means being a virgin or being a sexual athlete—you don't have sexual freedom. Sexual freedom comes ONLY when you can decide for *yourself,* because *you* are a sexual being, what you are going to do. When *you* decide not to hop into bed with everyone who comes along and asks you, when *you* decide that you can initiate your own sexual relationships, when *you* decide to abstain altogether, then you have sexual freedom.

Often that freedom has replaced the pre-pill problem of pregnancy with other questions and problems: With whom will you have sexual relations? Will it be a personal experience? Are you being the person you want to be? The very freedom from pregnancy brings problems of deciding that cause anxiety for both girls and boys. In other words, sex is more personally complicated and involved than technology and technique.

Depersonalized sex is also a problem for teen-agers. Many girls have gone along with the sexual style of the times. They have found it easier to go along, to ignore their own feelings, than to object. Not to get involved emotionally with sex creates apathy. And apathy, says psychotherapist Rollo May, author of *Love and Will,* is the opposite of love. Depersonalized sex is created by sex without feelings. And sex without feelings alienates people from their bodies in a way that they lose their ability for intimate relationships, explains Dr. May.

You are a sexual being before anyone asks you to share a sexual relationship. You are a sexual being whether you are asked or not. You are the one who must deal with sexuality, depersonalized sexual relationships, intimate relationships, contraceptives, sex instead of intimacy, and abortions. The biological facts about male and female differences or likenesses, or enjoyment or needs or interest in sexual life, do not decide for you what you will do sexually.

Sexual decisions can't be made by persons according to our masculine society's rules of what a girl does. Regardless of a particular man's perception that a woman is his sexual object, regardless of your perception of the worth of your body, regardless of your understanding of sex techniques for the most number of orgasms—there isn't a rule that answers your question of sexual behavior for you. There isn't a prescribed way that you can deal with your sexuality. There isn't an "all right way" that, because of scientific advancement in the prevention of pregnancy, can make your decisions for you. These decisions can produce as much conflict for you as sexual decisions did *with* the fears of pregnancy. One difference now is that you get little sympathy, or understanding or help, because many parents and other adults have decided that there are no problems in sexuality now that the problem of pregnancy has been solved! The visibility of a pregnant daughter is quite different from the visibility of a daughter who is having depersonalized sexual relations without feelings and without intimacy.

You cannot decide your sexual behavior by rules;

you can decide only by who you are. All your understanding about your sexuality must be integrated into your understanding about everything else about you. Especially the kinds of friendships you want right now and how these friendships support or don't support you, encourage or don't encourage you.

Relationship Choices

~~~~~~

Learning for Friendship

MARGARET MEAD

*One of the marvelous rewards of the women's move-
ment is friendship. Female solidarity, reaching out to
help our sisters, sounds so easy and natural. But many
women are too busy competing against one another for
dates and husbands and the boss's attention to notice
that they, like many men, don't value female ideas, opinions, or friendships.*

*Added to this is the myth that men are so much more
interesting, stimulating, intelligent, and well informed
than women. Decision and policy making, the best jobs
and highest money, belong mostly to men. This gives
women the false idea that if they identify with other
women, they are losers, and who wants a loser for a
friend?*

*You have no doubt heard the complaint that the only
things woman talk about are babies and recipes. Have
you ever thought to ask the question, What's so great
about men who talk only about sports and sex? The
point is that the interesting, stimulating, intelligent, and
well informed are* people—*and some of them are
women people.*

*Society's inequities against women make them feel
like nobodies. Nobody would rather be friends with
somebody. With the women's movement, gone are the
days when a group of high school women would plan*

to go to a movie on Saturday night—unless a guy asked them for a date and they automatically cancelled the movie with the nobodies. Gone are the days when any male (somebody) is better to be seen with than any female (nobody). Women are encouraging everyone to stretch beyond sex-stereotyped expectations of friendship. We are learning that girls and women really are interesting, bright, creative, innovating, and fun to be with. We are learning that males are more than potential dates, lovers, and husbands. We are learning that women are somebodies. Somebodies have and are friends.

"High school friendships," writes Dr. Margaret Mead, the well-known anthropologist, "will make you readier to explore the world."

Some people think of high school as the end of school, and some people think of it as the beginning of all sorts of things—college, technical training, work, marriage. The contrast in the way people think about it is illustrated by the word *commencement,* which means both graduating from something and starting something else. But whichever way you think about it, and whether the high school years are very enjoyable or a steady grind, they are the years when you are learning to form your own life style, deciding how you want to relate to other people, boys and girls, older people like teachers and coaches and counselors, younger kids, groups of people in which you may find that you are good at leading or better at carrying out other people's plans, or that you always know the words if somebody else can just carry the tune. It's the time when you find out whether you are at your best in the early morning (whether it's writing a theme or taking an early-morning swim) or at night—after everyone else is in bed.

So in a way the high school years, especially the senior high school years, are a kind of a rehearsal or learning time for life. The audience isn't there yet, and

you haven't your full costume on. You are all in it
together, each one learning his or her part, and it
isn't only your own success or failure that matters.

Your later hopes and expectations are going to be
shaped too by what happens to the others: by your
anxiety about the girl whom nobody seems to get on
with, your sorrow for the boy who is run over and
crippled for life, your wonder why you and one of the
girls you liked best never became friends. The clubs
and teams, the expeditions and camping trips, the
parties and picnics that you go on are all the setting
for this kind of exploration of what is a congenial life
style for you: When do you like to be alone and think?
When do you need to talk things over, not just think
them over? When do you feel left out and when do you
feel as if there just isn't anything that you can do?
When do you want to feel like the others, and when do
you want to feel that you are an absolutely unique
person—that no one in the whole world has ever been
so happy, or so miserable, as you are? If you want to
feel unique, you'd better not read any poetry that
week; but if you want to know how others have felt,
then a poem by Edna St. Vincent Millay or Emily
Dickinson may make you feel that other people have
known what you are feeling this minute. I remember
being very puzzled when I was in high school, reading
a line, "Now that love is dead, I am free to love again."
I couldn't think what that meant. But Edna Millay's

> We were very tired, we were very merry—
> We had gone back and forth all night on the ferry.

seemed something that made more sense.

Another thing that makes high school a time of rehearsal, and not yet the real play, is that you are still
living at home. Even if you go to boarding school, or
to camp for a whole summer, or on some expedition
to another country, you are still living at home. That
is where the money you live on comes from, that is
where you keep your things, the walls of your room

are where you stick up the pictures of people you like —this week—and where the pictures of someone you admired last year is half crooked because the Scotch tape has dried. When you start out for anywhere— school, a party, to visit someone else—you start from home. And afterward when you come back, triumphant or with feelings ruffled, cross or rebellious. Home is where you relate your victories, and nurse your wounds, scratched knees, a horrid pimple, too much sunburn.

In the way you fix up your room—the pictures you choose, whether you keep it neat or like a dump— you are rehearsing for the kind of home you will have some day, your own room at college, an apartment you share with other girls later, or, if you marry, the kind of house you want to have. All of these will have to be shared with someone else—perhaps someone with very different tastes—someone who is crazy about books or someone who thinks books just collect dust, some- one who likes mobiles better than blown-up pictures of the latest group of rock singers. But if you have thought out what your own taste is, why you have those little glass animals or china horses still about, whether you really want that huge face of a singer whose name you have forgotten staring down from the ceiling, it will be useful later, when there is just one wall space to argue over and compromise about.

In the same way, making friends is a rehearsal. Be- cause you find that a particular girl or a particular boy seems to be the most wonderful person you have ever met—or ever will meet—you can spend a lot of time getting acquainted and exploring just how well you do get along together. You don't have to sign a lease for a house tomorrow morning, or, as you will in college, have to put up with a too hastily chosen roommate for a semester. You still go home to sleep most nights, and if you visit other people's houses, both families get involved. So again it's rehearsal.

High school is a time for making friends. Of course some girls make friends much earlier and keep their kindergarten friends all their lives, but often childhood friends are just the children who lived next door, or the children of your mother's and father's friends, and not your own choice. And in elementary school there isn't as much choice to make. High school widens out —there are more people to choose among, and more kinds of people. The basic thing about friendship is that it is a matter of choice. Parents, brothers and sisters, aunts and uncles, nephews and nieces, and later, sons and daughters, are just there, for you to love or put up with, be thankful for, or give up on. But friends are the kind of compensation that life offers for all the lack of choice a family offers. In a family you may wish you were the oldest, or the only girl, or the youngest, or a twin; but wishing won't do you any good. But when you pick a friend you can pick someone who is a little older and more mature, or a little younger who will turn to you for help and advice, or someone just like yourself who will understand exactly how you feel about everything. You can pick someone who is always cheery and optimistic, or someone who puts a brake on your own impulsive optimism. And the other side of the picture is that the person who you pick as one of your friends has a choice too. In a family you may adore your older sister and want to spend a lot of time with her, but she may be burdened with the knowledge that, after all, she didn't pick you. But friends choose each other, try each other out, don't have to go too fast at first, don't have to promise to have lunch together every day from now to eternity. And each step can be delicious, finding out that you went to the same summer resort when you were six, that you both like to eat pickled walnuts, that neither of you catch poison ivy, that both of you secretly hope to be lawyers.

Friends like these are usually, in America, members of your own sex. Boys are making the same kinds of friends with boys. Especially in the early years of high school (and junior high school), both girls and boys really have more to say to another girl, or another boy, than they do to someone of the opposite sex. Girls mature faster than boys, and are often ahead of them in school, and both boys and girls mature at different rates. So the girl who is very mature for her age or the girl who is still very slight and small may be much happier with a girl of about the same size and state of maturity, who can play the same games well, or likes to talk about the same things, or share the same grievances about being given too much responsibility because they look so big, or not allowed to do things because they look so small.

And another important thing. You have to learn to make friends, to choose, to take the slow steps into a friendship, to learn how to understand what someone, who doesn't belong to your family and have the same family jokes, really means—to give and take on some sort of reciprocal basis, to listen when she wants to talk, if you expect her to listen when you do. In a family, you have to learn to accept the others as they are, talkative or quiet, fun or no fun, but in a friendship it's something you have chosen yourself—and you can develop it as you want it to be.

And once you know how to make friends, you can go on making friends all your life, wherever you go, without feeling unfaithful to your old friends. For friendship isn't like a love affair, in which thoughts of someone else are intrusive and give a lover a sense of infidelity. People with a gift for making friends make new friends all through their lives—and keep the old ones. They've learned how. When you are separated from close friends, they are someone to write to, perhaps about things you have no one else to talk to; years afterward when you meet again you find you can begin just where you left off, you have so much in common to refer back to and laugh about all over again.

Right now, in the 1970s, we are in the middle of a change in the life style of young people. This is partly due to the search for new ways of life which won't be so artificial and won't use up so much energy and so many of the irreplaceable materials that this planet is running out of, and it is partly due to changing attitudes toward marriage. We are coming out of a period when every girl—and so every boy—was being pressured by the whole society, by what their mothers said and how the school life was organized, to make marriage choices very young, and marry as young as possible. Of course many people didn't want the boys to get married as much as they wanted the girls to get married. But if marriages are to be between partners who are almost the same age—as is the fashion in the United States—then it followed that if all the girls were to get married young, then all the boys had to get married young too.

In this atmosphere of a frantic search for someone to marry, dating began in high school. It wasn't surprising that parents were anxious that their sons and daughters should associate only with young people who, they felt, would make suitable mates. So cliques were formed in high school among young people of about the same socioeconomic group, the same religion, the same ethnic group. In large high schools there might be great diversity of background, but the students themselves didn't benefit from it very much. Instead there would be groups of young Catholic Italian-Americans, or of young black Americans, of boys and girls of Jewish background, of Puerto Ricans, of different kinds of Protestants depending upon which Protestant church was the most prestigious in the community. Often these cliques, or crowds, came from the same part of the city, or lived in the same more or less exclusive suburbs. Often they had gone to elementary school together and simply continued these ties in high school. Each of these crowds tended to have a center, formed by the more active and assertive students. Sometimes there were fraternities and sororities in high school, and of course they increased the way each group selected people just as much like themselves as possible. In between these various cliques were the loners, the students who didn't quite fit any one of the styles: boys who were smaller or taller than the other boys, girls who were fat, or too immature, who hadn't learned how to move and dress like the others. Inside the crowds there were a lot of lonely people too, but they didn't look lonely to each other and they had to pretend they weren't, even to each other. As dating was the main activity, girls couldn't cooperate with each other very much because there was nothing to cooperate about. Even double dating wasn't very safe. Dances changed, and if a boy took a girl to a dance they danced together all evening, instead of cutting in as was the style in your grandparents' day, or having elaborate programs where it was the date's duty to get the girl he took a whole series of partners.

I am describing these old customs in this much detail because when older people think about high school dances these are the things they knew about. If the kind of style that your high school has today is different, they will still see it through their own memories. When I think of a dance, if I think of how I felt at thirteen, the one point was to dance with as many boys as possible. I always used to count the boys with whom I danced. As I grew older, it was a question of whether I liked the boy who took me very much, and then, instead of graciously saving the first and last dance for him, I'd suggest saving all the waltzes.

But there were and are lots of drawbacks to so much emphasis on dating in high school. It cut girls off from other girls, and boys off from other boys. If there were to be enough dates to go around, a lot of people had to date someone they didn't like very much . . . rather than be left out. Those who didn't fit got left out of the good times. It became stylish to like just one kind of music and to wear just one kind of clothes. Girls whose families couldn't afford the money for those clothes, or who couldn't find work to pay for them, dropped out of school. High school became—and still often is—a place where a girl was so busy keeping up with the others, others usually very much like herself, that she didn't have a chance to find out whether she might enjoy other kinds of people and do other kinds of things. In fact high school, with its dates and basketball games and hurt feelings and petty triumphs, became very much like the adult society that it mirrored. Young people were being got ready to be grownups as much like their parents and aunts and uncles as possible.

A lot of this is changing now. Young people do more things in groups—the kind of groups where you don't have to have a date to go. They gather together to listen to music, argue about ideas, make plans for expeditions, share a lot of things. Early marriage is not as fashionable as it was. Girls today are learning that they can plan for careers of their own, and try them out. They don't feel that they have to start going steady so young, or be pinned, or get engaged immediately. Mothers are relieved that their sons won't get married too young and let them alone more, to fool around with complicated electronic equipment or go fishing together.

This new atmosphere will give you a chance, many chances, which you wouldn't have had even ten years ago. You can take advantage of the fact that your high school draws on all kinds of communities, rich and poor, Catholic and Protestant, people whose ancestors came from many different parts of the world. As you don't have to spend all your time trying to find someone to marry, you don't have to belong to tight little cliques of suitable people to marry. You can make friends with very different kinds of girls, and find out what it is like to live in a family much richer or poorer than yours, and how differently people behave who live in houses that look the same on the outside. You will have more time to talk to girls about how you feel and what you want to do in life because you won't be competing for boys all the time but instead thinking about what you want to do in life besides getting married and having babies.

And you can make friends with boys too, boys you don't date and don't want to date. But if you do things together—put on plays, edit the school paper, go on a trip—you can explore each other's minds and find out how boys have learned to think about things in different ways than the way girls have learned to think. Many girls don't have any brothers, and many boys don't have any sisters. Yet in today's world men and women are going to have to work together, with sometimes one and sometimes the other in a higher position. If you learn to be friends with boys in high school, you can get on with men better in the working world.

Finally, high school is a good place to begin learning to leave home, to sleep in different kinds of houses, eat different kinds of food, get on with people who have very different habits. Up to high school, you don't go away from home much except to visit people just like your own family, people who brush their teeth the same way and eat the same cereals. High school is the place to begin to explore, to go on camping trips, to travel as much as you can, to break the ties to home that make you afraid to go other places. If you go to college, it will be a big help to have practiced being on your own with people you didn't know before. You can learn to recognize homesickness for what it is, memories of childhood and how comfortable and wonderful it was, which come to smother you with misery when you are among strangers, eating strange food. If you go away from home bit by bit, make friends with new people, all kinds, sleep in sleeping bags and stretchers and hammocks and whatnot, you'll be readier to explore the world.

High school is for rehearsing and learning. Now is the time to start making all kinds of friends and learning to enjoy all kinds of people.

MORE BOOKS BY MARGARET MEAD

The following are just a few of the many books by Margaret Mead. They have been selected for their relevance for you.

People and Places. New York: Bantam Books, 1963.
Culture and Commitment: A Study of the Generation Gap. New York: Morrow, 1970.

Blackberry Winter: My Earlier Years. New York: Morrow, 1972. An autobiography.

A Rap on Race (co-authored with James Baldwin). Philadelphia: Lippincott, 1971.

Growing Up In New Guinea. New York: Dell, 1970.

A Marriage Choice

JEAN STAPLETON

Jean Stapleton, an active NOW member on the national task force of Marriage, Family Relations, and Divorce, teaches journalism at East Los Angeles College in California. More important for this chapter, she is a loving and happy partner in an equal-partnership marriage!

Marriage is not spending your energy trying to trick your spouse into getting what you want, as shown on most TV situational comedies. Marriage is the delight of finding a person with whom you truly can be yourself. Decisions in marriage should be made on the uniqueness of the man or woman rather than on the role of husband or wife. Especially in our culture where the role of wife often means the major responsibility for all domestic work and child raising, regardless of a woman's interests and abilities in either of these areas. Ms. Stapleton describes marriage as a deep human relationship that, because it is a visible commitment to society, can free both partners to grow in whatever directions they value.

What is marriage, anyway? Is it the happy ending to a Hollywood romance, the happily-ever-after to a fairy tale? Does the marriage ceremony mean the end of loneliness, conflict, and unhappiness? Is it the beginning of a life of constant attention, praise, and fulfillment in parenthood?

Or is marriage a dying institution, one that traps both husband and wife in a dull, lifeless union which lasts until one of them dies or gathers the courage to ask for a divorce? Does the marriage ceremony mean the death of freedom, love, and excitement? Is it the beginning of a life of boredom, indifference, and a constant round of dirty diapers and dishes?

The answer, of course, is neither of these extremes. Marriage can be the deepest of human relationships and, as such, it shares much with other close relationships you have experienced—those with parents, brothers and sisters, and friends. But because it is deeper, its joys can be more joyous and its miseries more miserable. And because it is a *human* relationship, it will be neither all joy nor all misery.

Marriage is a partnership between a man and a woman. A healthy marriage is based on love, not necessity. It is two people choosing to make a life together because they want to, not because they have to out of economic or psychological weakness.

The person who marries for money usually gets just that—money—and an obligation to do what the partner with the money wants to keep the source of supply. The person who marries out of fear that she cannot cope with the world and must marry someone who can cope has a doomed marriage because marriage does not make things simpler—it makes them more complex. Not only must the outside world be dealt with, but it must be done in way that suits both partners, and the relationship between them must be maintained.

To handle the complexities, the partners need to be growing toward maturity, people with enough experience to be working toward knowing who they are and what they want out of life. If they are not at that point in life, then they certainly will not find their identities in marriage, where drastic change may end the marriage.

In many young marriages, neither partner is really

ready to face the world as an adult, much less as an adult marriage partner. That is one reason why the divorce rate among teen-age marriages is more than twice as high as for marriages generally.

Another reason is that teen-age marriage is often the result of the girl being pregnant, which brings the heavy responsibilities of being parents of an infant before the couple has quite adjusted to being marriage partners themselves. And young marriages are often made with little money. "We'll live on love" may sound romantic, but it leads to dissatisfaction and quarrels over how to use the couple's funds, increasing the chances of divorce.

Recently there has been a good deal of discussion in the press and on radio and television that marriage is a dying institution. Many people are living together without marriage and openly admitting it. Some of them are practicing a form of trial marriage, planning a wedding ceremony if they see that the relationship works. Others say they will never marry, that marriage is bankrupt, as shown by the fact that almost one out of three marriages ends in divorce. They believe it is none of society's business whom they live with, and none of society's business if they want to end the relationship.

What many people do not realize is that living together is the earliest form of marriage, and that all forms of marriage are done in a relationship to society. Legal marriage grants formal recognition to a couple's desire to be treated as a couple, a recognition many living-together couples say they want from society.

Living together has one advantage over marriage in that it is easy to dissolve—one person simply moves out. But that is also a disadvantage in that it is too easy and may be resorted to over small problems which could have been—and should have been—worked out. Aside from its lack of permanency, living together is much like marriage, with both its faults and its advantages.

The commitment of marriage, which makes it difficult to walk out of, also has its advantage. The fact that the partners intend to remain together and publicly promise to do so obligates them to work out differences and frees them to have a depth of relationship which is impossible in a temporary arrangement.

Perhaps that is why so many couples who begin by living together eventually marry, and why marriage, far from being a dying institution, is more popular today than ever. More than 90 percent of all women in the United States eventually marry, and 62 percent of women over sixteen are presently married and living with their husbands, an all-time high.

Our culture expects a great deal of marriage. Couples are supposed to be compatible and satisfy each other's needs for sex, money, a comfortable home, parenthood or nonparenthood, recreation, social contacts, intellecual and aesthetic companionship, and emotional support.

With this unrealistic expectation of marriage, the surprising thing is not that one in three marriages fail, but that two-thirds of marriages succeed! Divorce is no longer considered a disgrace; and it is no longer made almost impossible to obtain as it was in 1900, when only one out of twelve marriages ended in divorce. Today most couples who are unhappy eventually divorce. Of couples whose marriages do not end in divorce, about 80 percent consider themselves "happy" or "very happy" according to a *Life* magazine survey in November 1972.

No one, of course, marries with the expectation that the marriage will end in divorce. But many people marry with the expectation that happiness will come automatically, along with the rings and wedding gifts. The truth is, the foundation for a happy marriage is begun during the dating and engagement periods and must be constantly attended to during the marriage, especially in the first year.

The early years of dating serve to allow young people to get acquainted with the other sex, find out what they want and don't want in a future mate, and learn how to relate to a potential partner. Later dating becomes, consciously or subconsciously, a process of mate selection. A couple dates until it is obvious to one or the other that there is no future in the relationship, then it is discarded.

When a decision to marry is made, a couple spends their engagement exploring each other's interests, attitudes, family traditions, and expectations in depth.

After the marriage ceremony, a couple does not just relax and enjoy their relationship. They must learn how to solve their conflicts constructively, keeping communication between them open because, no matter how well-suited they are to each other, there will be conflicts ranging from the trivial (eating habits, where to keep things) to the major (where to live, when to have children).

One of the first concerns of many newly married couples is establishing who will be the boss—without first considering whether a "boss" is needed. Traditional wisdom says a man should be the boss and that, if he does not take a firm hand, the woman will usurp his role. This concept of marriage is that of rivals fighting over power. It has little to do with two people who love each other and who freely choose to be together. A boss is someone who imposes his or her will on an underling, someone who always has the final say. In a marriage no one should be taken advantage of and told what to do—no loving partner would want to treat his or her mate that way.

Marriage should be a partnership of equals, with decisions made jointly or taking turns for responsible decisions in the areas one knows most about. A corporation must designate a person with ultimate authority because it is large and complex and people are involved for profit, not love. But marriage involves two people who love each other and each is concerned that the other is getting fair treatment.

How do decisions get made without a boss? Usually two people who are compatible enough to marry have similar values and backgrounds. Most of the time they will be naturally in close agreement about decisions. If they are not in agreement about something, they will try persuading each other, each setting out all the reasons why his or her suggestion should be accepted. If either is persuaded, the problem is solved. If not, they must compromise. That becomes one of the most creative parts of marriage. Instead of acting on the first solution offered, the couple must think of all possible solutions and decide which one both can live with. It may seem as if this is a complex way to make decisions, but it is really less disruptive than letting one person have his or her own way. If one person decides, the other will resent it, may even sabotage the decision so he or she can say, "I told you it wouldn't work," and may become involved in trickery. It puts marriage partners in the role of adversaries instead of lovers and often leads to the death of all that is good in the marriage.

You've seen it all on television for years. At the beginning of almost any situation comedy the husband puts his foot down about something the wife wants to do. She then spends the rest of the show using tricks, tears, and/or bribery to get her way, and finally does, or else becomes convinced that he was right after all. But the creativity goes into the tricks, not into finding alternative solutions; and the person who was once thought of an ally before marriage now has become the enemy always trying to prevent the mate from being happy.

In the best marriages, husband and wife work as a team. The important thing is that the team gets ahead, no matter what the game. Every player does as much as possible to see to it that the team wins. Each player contributes what he or she does best. In a marriage it is important that the couple or family has enough money; that the house is reasonably clean and meals are cooked; that the children are cared for; that all the necessities of life are taken care of. It does not matter who does these things, but that they get done and in a way that both partners consider fair and reasonable. It is important that these things get done as quickly as possible so that each partner will have time for enjoying the other and their children, reading and studying, participation in the community, in sports and hobbies, and whatever helps each to grow.

The assumption that the man must be the boss is part of an old idea of marriage that expected certain behavior from each person based on sex alone. A husband was to earn the living, do the yardwork, initiate sex, handle financial matters, and fix anything that needed fixing. A wife was to clean the house, cook, shop, and raise the children.

This type of sex-role delineation left no room for individuality. It made no allowances for a person's interests, skills, likes, dislikes, and amount of time available. That a woman ruined everything she tried to cook made no difference—as the wife must cook. That a man was an excellent cook made no difference—he was to stay out of her kitchen.

Modern couples no longer need divide their chores by sex. They know that the best cook should do most of the cooking, that it often takes two salaries to live the way they want to live, that *nobody* likes to do some of the jobs. If she likes to cook but hates vacuuming and he likes vacuuming but dislikes cooking, they each take the chore they like. If both like to garden, they do it together on the weekends. Problems will arise most likely with the jobs both hate. Those jobs are the one each may try to say "belongs" to the other sex, as with the couple who wrote the advice columnist to ask, "Is it the man's job or the woman's job to take out the garbage?" The answer is that it is the couple's job; they must decide whether one of them will do it, if they will alternate or do it together, or, if they can afford it, hire it done.

Like other aspects of marriage, sex is a team effort— it takes the interest of both partners to make a good sex life. That means that the woman as well as the man takes the initiative for making love when she feels like it. A man can be enticed into wanting sex even though he originally was not interested, and a woman learns how, just as a husband learns how to seduce his wife.

Part of the traditional expectation about marriage is that women don't work—they stay home and their husbands take care of the breadwinning. In fact, 42 percent of women work, and 37 percent of married women work. On the other hand, about 10 percent of American husbands do not work at all—they are students, retired, unemployed, or disabled.

Motherhood itself is a part-time job, and a temporary job at that. A woman does not spend twenty-four hours a day being a mother. If she did, her children would grow up very unhealthy and overprotected.

The average woman has only two children, the last when she is about twenty-six. When she reaches her thirties the children are in school all day, and when she is in her forties they begin leaving home. That leaves her with some twenty years of unemployment before she reaches retirement age, if she considers her profession "full-time" mother.

A perceptive girl, even if she wants motherhood to be the focus of her early adult life, will plan ahead and train for a career. She will want to fulfill her life through her work as well as through her marriage, and she will be ready to share the burden of supporting the family just as she will expect her husband to share parenthood.

Tasks of parenthood should be shared even more than others because children thrive on having both parents involved with them. People who like children well enough to have them will want to share the satisfactions of watching a baby grow into a child and a child into an adult. Our society often tells men that children are for women only, but truly mature men ignore this. They know that the man who says "I don't like babies, I'll wait until my daughter is old enough to swim and then I'll get involved doing sports with her," will never be as involved as the father who starts his involvement with the baby.

Raising children can be as much a shared task as any other aspect of marriage. Either sex can diaper, bottle-feed, dress, bathe, or soothe an infant. Either can tie shoes for, transport, pack lunches for, discipline, or listen to an older child. A person of either sex who thinks children are important enough that he or she becomes a parent should think they are important enough to spend time with.

Parenthood, however, is not an automatic part of marriage. Many couples today see marriage as an end in itself. They want a close relationship with another adult, but they believe children will take time and energy away from that primary relationship and can even be a threat to the marriage. Increasingly, women decide that they want to be married but they don't want the major responsibility for child-raising which is what they would get with the particular man they plan to marry.

Others just do not like children. If you are not cut out for parenthood, or you want to give your full energy to your work, you will resent the children who take you away from it. They are expensive; they demand attention just when you don't want to give it to them; you will find it boring to discuss kitty cats and trains instead of your own interests.

If you enjoy children and decide to become a parent, you will find great rewards in watching a person develop from a helpless infant to an independent human being; you will have a close, loving relationship not only with the one person to whom you are married, but to a number of little people as well; and you will find that they give as much as they take in fresh insights, humor, warmth, and even, as they grow, in help with family responsibilities.

In any event, having children should not be left to chance. Whether to have them, how many, and when are deliberate choices to be made by a couple together, just as they make other major decisions.

One of the major decisions to be made by any couple is where to live. Traditionally, the couple has lived wherever the husband can best fulfill his career plans, but that isn't the only consideration for today's couples. This too is a team decision in which the couple weighs the factors of career opportunities both the husband and wife can find in a new town, whether they like the new location, whether it is worth it to give up their old friends, and whether it is more or less expensive to live in than their present residence. As more women get good opportunities for high-level jobs and advancement, increasingly the decision will be initiated by her good job offers; and the same consideration must take place for both partners.

The law often works against partnership in marriage. In many states it says that the husband will decide where the couple will live and how to spend their money. Many dated laws still on the books state that a married woman cannot make contracts, must do the housework, must be supported by her husband, must be available to her husband as a sexual partner at all times. Such laws have no effect on a happy marriage—the couple makes its own rules. It is only in a divorce proceeding or in an unhappy marriage that a couple uses these laws instead of working things out together.

In fact, a happy marriage is one that is not rigid— no strict rules or duties or roles to play according to sex. It is one that changes according to the needs and the personalities of the partners.

Most people assume that one of the laws of marriage which must be obeyed is that the woman must automatically change her name to that of her husband. In many states there is no law that requires her to do so, and in states with such a law she can go to court and usually retain her own name. Why would a woman choose to buck tradition and keep her own name? Because a name is part of you, something you identify with from birth, setting you off from the reputation you made under your single name. Former friends find it difficult to contact you. You may marry several times in a lifetime, each time cutting yourself off from the past and each time having to learn a new answer to the question "Who are you?"

And why? Because marriage changes you so much that you need to change your name as a symbol? Yes, marriage does change people, but it changes men, too, so why do they keep their names? What the name change really signifies in our society is the old English common law which stated: "The husband and wife are one person in law; that is, the very being or legal existence of the woman is suspended during the marriage, or at least is incorporated and consolidated."

The change of name is symbolic of the woman's legal ceasing to exist or being incorporated—her death as a legal person. More and more couples are rejecting that idea, just as they reject the unfair laws based on that common-law principle. Some of these couples each keep their own names; some hyphenate their two names and both use them; and some make up a new name that has significance to both.

Marriage by the traditional rules and expectations could be the straightjacket many people fear it will be. It could take away freedom of choice and stunt an individual's growth as she or he tried to conform to an unnatural role.

But couples who have equal-partnership marriages know that they do not have to conform to culturally imposed sex roles in their marriages. Just as this applies to household and parenthood tasks, it also means that they do not have to conform to "masculine" or "feminine" personality roles.

Such a "masculine" role says a man must be aggressive, detached, logical, decisive, firm, and physically strong. A woman must be passive, emotional, vacillating, illogical, and physically weak. Experts in human behavior know that all human beings, regardless of sex, are capable of all these traits, depending on the circumstances; but tradition calls a man "effeminate" and a woman "masculine" if they do not conform to the personality attributed to their sex.

Couples who have freed themselves from stereotypes in their marriage can see each other as persons. A husband will be treated as a unique personality, not just a representative of his sex, as will a wife. The partners are free to be themselves and to develop new facets of their personalities, even if these would traditionally be considered traits of the other sex.

Just as people often try to conform to an expectation of "masculinity" or "feminity," so they also try to conform to an outside expectation of "grownupness." That is, they behave not as they feel, but as they think is appropriate for their age.

While marriage is certainly a serious business, the delight of a good marriage is not found in work roles or parenthood, but in finding a person with whom you truly can be yourself, a person with whom you can be almost as natural as you would be all alone.

Newlyweds are notorious for talking babytalk with each other, and most happily married couples play games, joke, and behave in private much as they did as children. It is this aspect of marriage that makes it a refuge from the concerns and problems of work and the society at large, as well as the responsibilities of parenthood. One of the "tasks" of the newly married is to break down the barriers between them, to learn to be natural and playful with each other. That evolves as an outgrowth of the relationship, but only if neither partner stands in judgment, saying, "That's foolish," or, "We shouldn't act this way—we're grown up." Learning to drop the pretenses of adulthood is gaining freedom through marriage.

There is freedom, too, in commitment, even though it would seem at first to be the opposite. Once a woman chooses a partner for life, she can become free to be friends with men in a way similar to her friendships with women. The flirtations and signals and games that single people use to encourage or discourage each other are gone, since she and her husband are both out of circulation sexually.

A good marriage should not lead to loss of freedom and stifling of growth, but to different freedoms and a new potential for growth. Mature marriage partners will learn that one person—even a spouse—cannot possibly be all things to the other. A good marriage permits both husband and wife to launch out in new directions toward other people and careers for their personal fulfillment. Launching out in new directions may seem frightening, with unknown consequences, unfamiliar territory, and no one to help you. But with a trusted spouse you can dare much more, knowing you have the love, support, and companionship of your partner and a place to come back to for sharing either your triumphs or your defeats.

GOOD BOOKS ABOUT MARRIAGE

MARRIAGE

G. BACH AND P. WYDEN. *The Intimate Enemy.* New York: Avon, 1968. How to fight fair in love and marriage.

G. BACH, R. DEUTCH, AND P. WYDEN. *Pairing.* New York: Avon, 1970. Thy dynamics of marriage.

D. FERME. *Responsible Sexuality—NOW.* New York: Seabury Press, 1971. A history of the treatment of women and marriage, especially by religion; a study of Swedish society; and a plea for equalitarian relationships between the sexes.

J. AND C. CLINEBELL. *The Intimate Marriage.* New York: Harper & Row, 1970. How to have a close marriage in which you truly know the partner rather than one in which you merely live in the same house.

T. HARRIS. *I'm Okay, You're Okay.* New York: Harper & Row, 1967. The complexities of human behavior made understandable through transactional analysis. See chapter 8, "P-A-C and Marriage."

HISTORY

S. DITZION. *Marriage, Morals and Sex in America.* New York: Bookman Associates (Twayne), 1953. The many movements and historical events and philosophies which come together to shape our idea of marriage.

LAW

L. KANOWITZ. *Women and the Law.* Albuquerque: University of New Mexico Press, 1969. Details of the more than 1,000 laws discriminating against women. See chapter 3, "Law and the Married Woman."

Beauty Choices

<hr />

How to Beat the Beauty Game

DONNA LAWSON

The women's movement has brought about radical change in personal style. Many women have said no to the beauty parlor, to shaving underarms and legs, to wearing all kinds of sprays, and to time and money spent on shopping and clothes for every time of day or event. Such women are comfortable wearing jeans and T-shirts, low-maintenance hair styles, and no makeup. If an outfit feels right, it can be worn all the time.

Anti-fashion becomes a style you can choose. But it isn't the only style, even for a liberated woman. Liberation sets you free to do things many ways. Freedom in personal style lets you choose what you wear for all kinds of reasons—not only because you are female and have to dress as the fashion industry dictates. You can choose to be the warmest person at the football game, the most actively dressed student at the picnic, or the most high-fashion dresser in school—the most anything! If you are really free, you can choose any style.

Clothes and style don't give you your values and commitments, they only help with what you already are. Developing a style can be like packaging. The package, your image, can be what you really feel, what you want to feel, how you want others to see you, or just happen with no thought at all. You can be chic, *cute, sophisticated, woodsy; you can dress like a blue-collar worker, a feminist, a model, a freak, a hippie, a girl athlete, or a sex object. Whatever your style, people react to it; they respond in different ways according to the image you give them.*

Remember the time you put something on, looked in the mirror, and couldn't wait to get it off? The look wasn't you, was it? Or the time you didn't bother to change even though something wasn't right for you, and you spent the whole miserable time self-consciously aware of yourself? Are you aware that your own style comes off very much like that of your closest friends? And how "others" look different from you and your friends? The style you choose for right now won't last forever. As you grow and change and learn about other kinds of people, other kinds of values, and other ways to look at the world, your personal style will change too.

Donna Lawson, newspaper editor, author, and feminist, has written several books on the subject of beauty and fashion. "Good posture, exercise, proper diet, tranquility are the backbone of good health and beauty," writes Ms. Lawson in this chapter.

In a liberated life, character and health count for more than candy-box good looks. In this life everyone can be beautiful in her own way. And getting yourself together is a cinch if you don't get hung up on the so-called feminine ways of going about it. Grooming and good health should fit into your day like eating and breathing. Making "cover-girl" beauty your total preoccupation could turn you into a mindless wonder. The idea is to look right for you and then get on with the business of life.

First principle—an out-of-shape body is bad news. In this state you feel bad and operate inefficiently. Sometimes we let our bodies go because we don't like them. But feeling fat isn't worth that kind of self-indulgence. There is too much life to live to be hampered with out-of-whack flesh and bones.

Bad posture causes all kinds of body problems. Sometimes young women who feel fat are merely suffering from weight that has shifted to all the wrong places. So, do a quick weight shift and see what happens. Pull head and neck up by your ears and watch chin and shoulders straighten. Pull hipbones slightly forward, pulling stomach in and rolling under rear. Relax knee joints. If knees knock inward, turn them ever so slightly outward. Place feet parallel. Slightly tighten area between big toe and outside of heel to pull up arches. Take a look. An amazing thing has happened to your body in a matter of minutes. You look thinner, straighter, and you feel more confident.

Along with good posture, your body needs exercise to keep blood, bones, nerves, and fatty tissues all working right. Exercise is good for you. Jogging and swimming work on the entire body. So does dancing. And yoga. And tennis. Exercise is as important to your day as food.

And food is important only if it's the right food. Some foods make you feel terrific. Others merely put on weight and drain your energy.

Good proteins, carbohydrates, fats, vitamins and minerals do more to make you beautiful than any cosmetic you could put on your face. Protein—in meat, fish, cheese, nuts, and grains—gives you strength and energy and repairs body cells that break down. Carbohydrates give you get up and go. But stick to fruits and vegetables; avoid the pastas, soft drinks, and sweets that store up in your body tissues and only fatten you up. Some fat is needed daily for energy, and for good skin, hair, and nails. Polyunsaturated fats are good— fish, seed and vegetable oils, all of which after heating stay liquid at room temperature. Saturated fats, like butter, chocolate, and animal fats, all harden at room temperature after being heated. They clog pores and arteries and blow you up in size.

You also need vitamins. For clear skin, shiny eyes and hair, and hearty nails, pack in vitamin A in fish, liver, eggs, whole milk, cheese, carrots, apricots, cantalopes, and dark green leafy vegetables. Vitamin B—in whole-grain cereals, organ meats, yogurt, green vegetables—gets you through life's stresses and strains. Vitamin C—in oranges, grapefruit, berries, tomatoes, and leafy green stuff—helps prevent colds, fights skin infections, and builds up teeth, gums, and the bones' connective tissues. Vitamin D—in sunshine, salmon, tuna, mackerel and other seafoods—helps prevent tooth decay and builds up bones.

Then there are the minerals. The calcium in milk products builds strong bones and healthy teeth and gums. Iodine, in all products of the sea, helps to regulate the thyroid which controls your metabolism. This in turn affects your weight and the way you feel. Iron —in liver, molasses, raisins, apricots, and egg yolks— raises your energy level and improves the skin's vitality. When you're low in iron your skin looks gray and lusterless. Phosphorus—in fish, dairy products, eggs, and lean meat—gives a glow to hair and skin. And some sources claim it makes you think faster and steadies your hand. Sulfur—in lentils, clams, eggs, and wheat germ—strengthens fingernails and livens hair.

All this, and one more, before you take a brush to your hair or color your cheeks. That all-important one more is relaxation. If you're uptight and tense it will show on your face, in the way you move and react. To find tranquility, to learn to ride through life's hassles, makes you lovelier inside and out.

So learn to live your own energy pattern. Try to get important things done when you're at your energy peak, and give in a little and do the routine jobs when you're not riding high. Catch yourself when things seem muddled. Don't work yourself into a state of confusion and anxiety. Put your projects in order of priority and do them one at a time as they come.

Make a list of your own personal energy stealers and try to eliminate them from your life. People who load up with their problems might be one drain. Or noise. Or biting off more than you can chew and always saying yes because you're so glad to be asked. Try to get rid of unnecessary hassles. Save time for yourself.

Watch your sleep patterns. Maybe another hour's sleep will make all the difference. Or perhaps you need catnaps, shorter spans of sleep rather than one long stretch. Get your head on a cushion, any place to grab a few winks when needed.

Quiet, too, should cool you out. Short times alone to reflect, to meditate, to set life straight can help you get through a lifetime of challenges and hurdles.

Good posture, exercise, proper diet, and tranquility are the backbone of good health and beauty. Cosmetics and clothes are frosting. They reflect the outside image you decide to show the world. The image should be maintained with ease at the cost in time, money, and energy you choose to give them.

Commercial cosmetics cost plenty. Advertising is always revving women up to buy, buy, buy: *Buy our product and you'll win your man and therefore be more worthwhile. Don't buy our product and you're a loser.* Lots of advertising money goes into feeding human insecurities. Stop playing into the game. It shouldn't be necessary.

You can make your own cosmetics just like great-grandma did. They're as good if not better than anything you buy in a jar. And they are much less expensive.

Over and over again, the same ingredients have appeared in natural beauty preparations: eggs, milk products, honey, bran, oatmeal, strawberries, and the herbs rosemary and chamomile. All can be bought at the local supermarket. Some of the natural ingredients, like lemons and vinegar, are fairly strong astringents. On the other hand, strawberries are milder. Bananas, avocados, and olive oil are emollients; they make skin and hair soft and supple. Bran reduces oiliness of skin and hair. Muslin bags of bran put into the bath reduces body oiliness. And when bran is brushed through your hair it serves as a dry shampoo.

Head to toe you can cover yourself in natural ingredients. You'll feel and look all the better for it. Feeling right and looking right, remember, go hand in hand. One ensures the other.

Start with a bath to soothe you inside and out. A salt bath works wonders. When you're worn and weary, take a cellar of salt to the bath with you. Pour half a box of salt into a tub of hot water and swish it around. In small circular motions, rub the rest of the salt over your body. Salt awakens tired dull skin and revives your spirits. It's also antiseptic and deodorizes your body naturally.

To clean and condition normal skin, use natural oils: safflower, corn, peanut, sunflower, almond, avocado, soybean or carrot. To condition dry skin, rub the inside of an avocado peel or a tomato slice over it. Old dead skin rolls off in small dirty flakes, leaving a smooth layer of soft, glowing skin. Like bran, oatmeal absorbs excess skin oil. Tie some into a square of cheesecloth and secure it with a rubber band. Soak under warm water tap. Then rub bag over skin. Let oatmeal dry on face for five minutes. Rinse off with warm water.

Cucumbers, watermelon slices, or grapes all can be applied to the skin as moisturizers. Homemade skin masks remove blackheads, dirt, grime, and dead skin. A ripe banana mask rubbed into skin and left fifteen minutes cleans and softens dry skin. A paste of oatmeal and milk spread over face for fifteen minutes removes excess dirt and oil.

For a hair rinse, chamomile—a quarter of a cup steeped in and strained from a quart of boiling water brightens blondes. And rosemary—two tablespoons steeped and strained from a pint of boiling water brings out natural brunette highlights. Don't rinse out either hair preparation.

Most young skin is so vibrant it needs little additional color. On the other hand, if wearing makeup makes you feel better about yourself, go ahead. Make it yourself. Simply spread a smear of vaseline or a bit of talc on a piece of glass. Then stir in a few drops of food coloring. Use colors straight or mixed together —yellow and red make an orangish lip gloss. Green, blue, turquoise, toast, and violet food coloring supply eye shadow.

Now that you have the cosmetic industry licked, try making your own clothes to save money and for the fun of designing and making your own.

You can buy a new sewing machine for $75 and a good reconditioned one for half that amount. Learn the basics of sewing on your own or sign up for a mini-sewing class offered in many high schools. If a high school sewing class won't work for you, check with your local YWCA about classes for your age group. If they don't already have what you want, maybe they would start sewing lessons if you and a few friends are interested.

Pattern companies offer an enormous variety of clothing styles from which to choose. The patterns are scaled to your measurements. But if you want to assure absolute accuracy, you can do as professional designers do and make a muslin garment first.

The garment can be cut and stitched together quickly using a sewing-machine basting stitch. Where adjustments must be made—widening the hips or narrowing the shoulders—extensions of muslin may be added or pieces of it cut out. This addition or subtraction process, utilizing a muslin sample, will give you a perfect pattern molded to your own specific body proportions, a pattern usable time and time again in new and different fabrics.

Wandering through a fabric shop is enough to encourage one to sew. There is a color, pattern, and style for every individual taste. In fact, one interesting way to establish your unique style is to pick a commercial pattern and then a fabric to unite with it. After you have learned to make rough muslins from commercial patterns, you'll soon catch on to making your own designs. By changing a neckline or a sleeve or a fastening on your "muslin," you are, in fact, making your own pattern.

And, one day, when you understand the workings of patterns and muslins well enough, you'll be able to cut your own patterns directly into the muslin without using a commercial pattern first. With a little practice and a lot of interest, you could make your entire wardrobe.

Actually, very few clothes are needed to make a useful and attractive wardrobe. More than anything, a good wardrobe takes planning. Your entire closet full of clothes should fit together like a jigsaw puzzle. Sew up new garments, or buy them—a skirt here, a vest there, a pair of shoes, a belt 'n' bag—to go with something you already have in your closet. Interchange your clothing. The more interchangeable parts the better—pants, skirts, vests, jackets, accessories can be combined in infinite ways.

Pick a basic color for the core of your wardrobe—your coat, skirt, pants—one that most enhances your skin, hair, eyes, and body build. About color, Arnald Scaasi, the outstanding high-fashion designer of New York and Paris, suggests that basic colors such as tan, navy blue, black, brown, and gray are serviceable, but there is always the exception to the rule. He says a bright red coat or any bright shade can become a basic coat color and end up being much more flattering than some of the darker shades. Choose your accessories in complementary colors. Remember, all your accessories need not match; they look better if they don't.

Say that green is your best color. Select a bright shade as a sample color for the core of your wardrobe. What are your basic needs and activities and what is the climate like most of the year where you live? These are the basic questions Scaasi asks when he designs a complete wardrobe.

You need not follow the mockup wardrobe below

as is, but it should give you some ideas to modify to your own style:

- A green coat
- A long wool cape in a bright color that goes well with green—magenta is nice
- A pair of well-fitted garbardine or wool pants in green or brown
- A long wool skirt in green, brown, or oxford gray, plaid or plain to wear with cape for evening
- A knit dress
- A short skirt in green, brown, oxford gray, or magenta
- A pair of well-fitted bluejeans
- A bluejean skirt, long or short
- A bluejean jacket—trim it with recycled fur around neck for a great look (all denim garments may be colorfully patched, painted with washable acrylics, embroidered—see my book *Superjeans* listed at the end of this chapter for more ideas)
- Tops—buy or make shirts; vests; turtle neck, crewneck, and cardigan sweaters; and several cotton T-shirts in colors to coordinate with pants and skirts, coats, and jeans jackets
- Accessories—bags and belts, shoes and socks, mittens and caps, and scarves and jewelry add a lot of life to your wardrobe; small and inexpensive changes in accessories make you feel as if you have a complete change in clothes

With a little ingenuity, you can beat the beauty game. You can make your own clothes and cosmetics, or buy what suits *your* personal style. You can choose to put yourself together uniquely and individually.

The way you face the world concerns you more than anyone else. After all, others can't face the world for you. Not your parents, not your teachers, not your man. No, baby. Just you. When you feel good both inside and outside about your own beauty, you will be free to move out actively toward the rest of the world.

BOOKS BY DONNA LAWSON

Beauty Is No Big Deal. New York: Bernard Geis, 1971.

Mother Nature's Beauty Cupboard. New York: Bantam Books, 1975. A book about natural cosmetics, selected as one of the Young Adults Library Books of the Year in 1973 by the American Library Association.

If You Can't Go Naked, Here's Clothes to Sew On Fast. New York: Grosset & Dunlap, 1973. Making your own clothes by wrapping, pinning, and almost no sewing skills is what the book is about.

Superjeans. New York: Scholastic Book Club, 1975. A book that tells all about how to decorate your favorite faded blues.

Turning-on Choices

Deciding about Drugs and Alcohol

ROGER F. AUBREY

Roger F. Aubrey, director of guidance and health education for the Boston suburb public schools of Brookline, works with, writes about, and is most concerned with high school students in the present-day American drug culture.

Dr. Aubrey describes why young people take drugs, how people are turned on and turned off from drugs, and how drugs affect your behavior. He writes that most people use mood-changing drugs for pleasure and fun. No one originally turns to drugs to increase their pain or to complicate their lives with more problems.

CASES OF DRUG TAKING BY YOUNG ADULTS

The first time Cheryl Winters tried drugs was sixteen years ago. She was given her first injection by a doctor, and it probably saved her life. At that time, Cheryl Winters was six months old and in a hospital with pneumonia.

The first time Nuni Longarrow tried drugs was on her fifteenth birthday. On that day, she and twenty other American Indians were initiated into the rite of peyotism by her tribe in the Southwest. Part of the initiation ceremony included the drinking of a tea made from the peyote cactus plant. The usual results from taking this drug are hallucination or distortions and alterations of consciousness.

Shirley Johnson has a hard time remembering her first drug experience. Shirley is a heroin addict and has been on the streets for years. Her first memory of drugs goes back to junior high school days. She used to skip school with friends and smoke marijuana and drink wine in boy friends' cars.

If alcohol is considered a drug (and it is, according to most medical experts), then Sue Wasserman has been taking drugs for most of her life. Sue's family usually has one or two glasses of wine with dinner each evening. Since she was a small child, Sue and her brothers and sisters have joined their mother and father on these occasions.

Jill Guthrie takes a drug every day of her life. However, few people are aware of her need for this drug. She usually takes this drug before each meal; if she doesn't, serious problems might occur. Jill suffers from a mild form of epilepsy and without this drug she might have seizures or convulsions.

With the exception of a few marijuana cigarettes, Sallie Bates had never entered her high school drug scene. At a graduation party, however, Sallie was given a cube of LSD by one of her friends. Sallie ended up in the emergency ward of a nearby hospital three hours later in a severe state of depression.

THE WIDE RANGE OF DRUGS

All the young women just mentioned are drug-takers. Each on more than one occasion has swallowed, sniffed, smoked, or had injected into her body a chemical substance changing the regular functioning of the brain and body. However, the main difference among these young women lies not in the fact that she takes alcohol or drugs. Rather, they differ because of the reasons behind their drug taking and the specific drug or beverage selected to fulfill this purpose.

With the exception of small children, most people in the United States sample a wide variety of drugs each year. In fact, we are encouraged to try many drugs including a variety of alcoholic drinks by advertisements on TV and radio, in newspapers and magazines, by advice from our friends, through the daily example of people around us, and by the easy availability of drugs and alcohol through legitimate and illegitimate sources.

The use of drugs in a broad sense includes all chemical substances taken into the body that cause changes in the physical and/or mental functioning of an individual. This broad definition includes such common substances as coffee, tea, cigarettes, beer, wine, hard liquor, aspirin and other headache remedies, nonprescription pills and liquids promising relief from pain or ease in sleeping, laxatives, birth-control pills, and so on. All these substances, and a great many more, are classified as drugs.

In a narrow sense, drug taking can be defined as the illegal or unlicensed use of a variety of drugs, including the use of alcohol by underage adolescents. Some of the drugs in this category may have a legitimate reason for being taken, for example, when they are prescribed by a physician. Included here would be such drugs as tranquilizers (to relieve tension and anxiety), amphetamines (to stimulate or awaken), and barbiturates (to produce sleep or sedation). Also included in this category are drugs with no real medical use (heroin, airplane glue), or drugs used by doctors only for experimental purposes (LSD).

This chapter examines drug taking in its narrow sense. Our main focus is on drugs and alcoholic beverages that produce changes in the moods, emotions, and behavior of persons. Our concern is therefore limited to a small number of drugs and narcotics. Alcohol is included because our definition of drugs includes alcohol. In fact, alcohol is the most widely used and abused drug in the history of humankind.

ARE DRUGS GOOD OR BAD?

The word "drugs" means many things to many people. Most parents and law-enforcement officers feel "drugs" are bad, and there should be strict laws regulating their use. On the other hand, medical doctors would say "drugs" are good and save thousands of lives each year. Students, too, differ on how they view drugs. Some students feel drugs such as marijuana, like beer, should be legalized and available to everyone above a certain age; other students agree with law-enforcement officers on strict penalties for all persons selling, buying, or using drugs.

Although most people have strong opinions about whether drugs and alcohol are good or bad, few individuals look beyond this question. Are drugs bad? Is it wrong for someone in pain to have the pain eased by a drug? Is it wrong for a mature person to take a chemical substance to increase pleasure and satisfaction if this act does not harm anyone else? Finally, is it harmful for someone to experiment with drugs in order to gain valuable knowledge and information about herself?

The answers to these questions are not as simple as they might appear. Questions and answers go well beyond the simple problem of whether drugs are good or bad. Instead of dealing with this endless debate, it seems more useful to deal with the actual behavior of individuals using and not using drugs and alcohol. In this way we can avoid labeling a drug good or bad, and instead discuss what occurs when a drug is abused or felt to enhance the behavior of a person.

Drugs, therefore, are not of themselves something wicked or evil. The problem with all drugs that are misused comes from the behavior of the person abusing the drug and not the drug itself. A person who drives a car recklessly after drinking too much alcohol is exhibiting poor judgment both in regard to her driving and because she overindulged herself with alcohol. Persons who abuse drugs have allowed drug use to overwhelm and restrict the direction of their lives. In particular, individuals called "drug abusers" have developed specific patterns of drug use that weaken their growth in social, vocational, career, spiritual, and personal areas.

WHO ARE THE DRUG USERS?

Most people in the United States are drug and/or alcohol users in one form or another. Many of us begin using drugs when we first wake up in the morning. We may take an aspirin for a headache or a vitamin or "pep pill" (amphetamine) to ensure a good day. Many people could not make it through the first hour of the day without a cup of coffee or a cigarette.

As the day proceeds, many individuals will take a morning laxative or perhaps a pain-killer to relieve a discomfort. Others will have a beer or cocktail with lunch, and some will smoke their first marijuana cigarette of the day. As lunch goes on, a great many people will pop a pill to aid their stomach in the digestion of food (or to deal with excessive gas and acidity). As night draws near, other patterns of drug usage appear. Some individuals literally live in a drug culture and use drugs throughout their every waking hour. They feel (and for some it may be true) they could not survive a full day without drugs.

Drugs are used and abused by millions of Americans. Recent estimates put the number of alcoholics in this country at approximately 9 million. Add to this figure well over half a million regular heroin users and the millions of Americans who could not function without sleeping pills, diet pills, laxatives, alcohol, pain-killers, caffein, and nicotine, and you have an idea of how many Americans use drugs regularly.

Drug users and abusers are not always easy to distinguish between. Someone dependent on a hundred-dollar-a-day heroin habit should be easy to spot. But an actress who uses sleeping pills the night before the opening night, and pep pills just before the play, may be harder to spot. For each, drugs have become a major part of their life.

WHY USE DRUGS?

Study after study has shown there is no single pattern or easy explanation for why people become dependent on drugs. For example, look at the following list of reasons for possible explanations of adolescent alcohol and drug taking. How many reasons could you add to this list?

Reasons for Adolescent Alcohol and Drug Taking

Alcoholic or drug-taking parents	Influence of others
Boredom with school and home	Inferiority feelings
Parents too easy and permissive	Rebellion against parents
Weakness of personality	Loneliness
Difficulty in getting along with others	Curiosity/adventure
Desire for new experiences	Escape from problems
Lack of love and affection	Emotional immaturity
Search for a sense of meaning	Enjoyment and pleasure
Moral and spiritual confusion	Pressure from school

Lack of goals and
     purpose   Desire to act grown-up

In looking over this list, you may have added a few
more reasons. In fact, you yourself may have tried
drinking alcohol or taking drugs for reasons other than
the ones on this list. Nevertheless, there are two reasons any drug taker would agree *are not* reasons for
why she turned to drugs. First, no one turns to drugs
to increase the amount of pain and frustration in their
lives. Second, no one *originally* turns to drugs to increase the amount of problems in their lives.

A PARTIAL EXPLANATION FOR
DRUG EXPERIMENTATION

The two reasons just mentioned are extremely important in understanding drug-taking behavior. Many
people take alcohol and drugs as a means for solving
problems. These problems may range from shyness in
meeting people to overweight to unhappiness and loneliness. The list could be endless. The important fact is
that drugs are seen by many people as a means of
solving or relieving problems.

A second major reason for drug taking was over-
looked for many years. Scientists, doctors, educators,
and parents simply couldn't accept the fact that many
people take alcohol and drugs because they gain pleasure and satisfaction. Drugs for many people today are
a means of social and recreational enjoyment. This fact
is especially hard for parents and adults to accept even
though many of them have used alcohol for years for
the same purpose. Today, these same parents have great
difficulty in accepting the fact that most doctors and
drug experts have placed drinking in the same category
as other drugs.

If we accept for a moment the simple explanation
that people take drugs partially to solve problems or
to ease discomfort and increase pleasure, we have some

chance of avoiding an argument. We also have a realistic way of examining the behavior of people who use drugs without making a judgment as to whether their behavior is bad or good. A woman out of work, recently divorced, and left with three small children should not be judged immoral or evil because she turns to alcohol to solve her problems and ease her pain. Even though her behavior may lead only to more serious problems, judging another person's behavior is not a helpful way to understand her present life conditions.

The idea that people take drugs in order to gain pleasure and satisfaction is extremely difficult for many people to accept. However, these same people would probably agree that eating an apple pie or pizza at a party is quite all right. Dancing or listening to music is probably another activity these people would approve of at a social gathering. The list of activities that are pleasing to individuals could be endless, but the point is obvious: *different experiences produce pleasure in different individuals. And for many people today, drugs and alcohol are an acceptable and pleasing form of social and recreational entertainment.*

TURNING ON AND TURNING OFF

Turning on and using drugs and alcohol is very easy today. Turning off must be seen realistically as a more difficult process, unless we deny the existence of millions of people who lead a nightmarish life because of their dependency on drugs.

The term "drug or alcohol dependent" is used by doctors and others to describe people who cannot function in society without the use of these substances. Drug- or alcohol-dependent people require daily amounts of these chemicals just to survive both mentally and physically. Without drugs or alcohol, these people would have to be hospitalized or placed in treatment facilities.

On the other hand, "drug or alcohol dependent" describes a particular kind of person who is prone or susceptible to these chemical substances. Individuals who are so labeled may never in their lives have taken a drink or a drug. Nevertheless, their unique personality makeup is such that they could quite easily become dependent or reliant on drugs. These people, once they begin taking drugs, have an excellent chance of ending up "hooked," or addicted.

There are two kinds of dependency on drugs. One is that which comes directly from the drug itself, *physical dependency.* People in this category develop in their body system an actual physical need for the effects of a specific drug or alcohol. Without regular and daily amounts of the drug, pain and discomfort are present. Complete withdrawal, removal of the drug (including alcohol), can cause extreme pain and suffering.

The other form is *psychological dependency.* In this case the person has come to rely on drugs as a means of dealing with life, people, and difficult situations. Instead of using inner strength and courage, the person has come to rely on drugs and alcohol to get through tough experiences. The effect of drugs has weakened and lessened the ability of the person to deal with an inner source of strength. Instead, a bottle or a pill must do the job.

The physically or psychologically dependent person has to be considered in any talk about drugs because none of us wishes to think of ourselves as potentially dependent. Those who never have taken drugs or alcohol can obviously say, "I've never done it so it can't happen to me!" At the same time, those who have tried drugs on various occasions, with no ill effects, can also say, "No, not me—I can turn off anytime I want." Finally, those really into drinking or drugs can say, "I can quit anytime I want. . . . Sure, I'm really into this thing now, but I wasn't always and I can really get clean anytime I want."

WHAT'S IN IT FOR YOU?

As a young adult, your chances of using alcohol and drugs are very high. For many reasons, teen-age drinking has increased rapidly in the last year. It is harder for most of you to decide what you are going to do about drinking because many of your parents drink, and they don't consider alcohol a "drug." And because alcohol is legal, it appears safer to you than other drugs. Let's go over some of the reasons others might bring up if they talk to you about alcohol and drugs. It is hardly fair to speak only of dependent or ill people using drugs when millions of persons use these same substances without becoming dependent.

One key reason already mentioned for using drugs and alcohol is pleasure. There is no way of denying that certain drugs add to a person's feeling of enjoyment and relaxation. Your personal choice to drink or to take drugs to increase pleasure and enjoyment can be a most important decision. Which drug or alcoholic beverage would you select for this purpose? How much of the drug or alcohol would you take? In what situations or with which people would you do this experimentation? Finally, how much do you know about the short- and long-range effects of this drug on your mind and body?

These questions may seem silly or unimportant to you. After all, you simply want to feel good or relaxed and this shouldn't involve a lot of questions or the reading of books. Taking a drink, popping a pill, or smoking marijuana just isn't that big a deal. Must you think and analyze everything you do just to have a little fun and enjoyment?

No, you don't have to question everything. It is your body, your life, your future, and your happiness. So long as you do not restrict the freedom of others or injure them, you have a tremendous amount of freedom. This is especially true in a drug culture such as ours that offers multiple drug experiences to individuals throughout their lifetime. However, because of this fact you should consider the following questions when you consider using alcohol or drugs purely for pleasure in social or recreational settings.

1. What do you know about the particular drug or alcoholic beverage? What category of drugs does it fall under? How does it affect the brain and the body?

2. How long do the effects of this drug or alcoholic beverage last? What minimal amounts of this drug bring about the effect you wish, and is there a danger in taking more than a specific amount of this drug?

3. What occurs when this drug or alcohol is mixed with another drug or alcoholic beverage? Does it increase the feeling you desired, or does it result in an entirely different feeling and sensation?

4. Are there legal penalties attached to the use of this drug or alcohol? If so, are these penalties enforced? What are your chances of being arrested?

5. Where will you be and who will be present when you take this drug or alcohol? Will these people help or protect you if the need should arise?

6. How much does the drug or alcohol block, distort, alter, or change your perception of reality? Does the drug or alcohol allow you to maintain sufficient contact with reality and not limit your capacity to deal with emergencies?

7. Is your choice of a drug or alcohol a substance that is an addictive chemical? In other words, have you selected a substance that over time could cause your body to require this chemical for daily functioning?

8. Do you have friends who have successfully used this type of drug or alcohol with no ill effects? If so, will they be present when you experiment?

9. What's in it for you? What kind of feelings do you
   wish to have as a result of taking this drug or alcoholic beverage? Why are these feelings important
   for you to experience?

DRUGS AND ALCOHOL FOR
PROBLEM SOLVING

Although today's use of drugs and alcohol for social
and recreational purposes is a new and unsettled issue,
the use of these substances for problem solving is quite
old. Of particular interest to women is the fact that in
this country in the late 1800s and early 1900s, the
largest number of opium addicts were women in the
20–40 age category. This problem began with the wide
distribution of patent and drugstore medicines following the Civil War. Women in small towns and farming
areas were the targets of peddlers and others selling
"medicines" that contained a mixture of opium and
alcohol.

The woman who purchased these patent medicines
was usually a person desiring some relief from the
fatigue of life in nineteenth-century America. These
patent medicines offered some help to the tired and
exhausted, but the price they paid was an addiction to
a powerful narcotic drug. This problem was resolved
eventually by the passage of the Pure Food and Drug
Act in 1906, which regulated the interstate sale of un-
safe and misbranded food and drugs.

Relief from pain, fatigue, and physical discomfort
is only one example of the use of drugs and alcohol
as a means of solving or aiding personal problems. In
fact, the use of drugs to aid in helping a person deal
with physical distress is easily understood. What is
often difficult to understand is the same use of drugs
and alcohol to solve problems arising from emotional
and social concerns.

Examples of people who use drugs and alcohol to

solve personal problems not related to physical reasons are numerous. Think for a moment of the number of friends and acquaintances you know who are somewhat shy, timid, or uncertain of themselves. What would they say if at a party you offered them something to make them more relaxed and at ease with other people? If they accepted some marijuana or a beer, it might very well relax them and make them more comfortable. The question is, would they then use these chemicals as a way of life whenever they felt uncertain of other people and situations? Would the drug or alcohol become in time a substitute for the "real" person they are or might have been?

Other examples of problem solving through drug and alcohol use could range from persons using "pep pills" to cut their appetites so they can lose weight, to unhappy and lonely individuals finding a secret fantasy world through drugs, to persons who wish temporary escape, to the unemployed, to shaky people with an unhappy past and an uncertain future. For all these people, and a great many more, drugs and alcohol hold some promise for getting out from under the pressures and tensions of life. They also shut out, for however short a period, the feelings we all have sometimes of helplessness, unhappiness, and inadequacy in certain situations.

The question all of us must face in using drugs and alcohol to solve personal problems is easy to say but difficult to recognize and resolve. The question is, "Do drugs and alcohol really assist us in dealing with personal problems or do they simply help us in getting around the problem temporarily?" If they don't actually aid us in handling personal problems, then an additional question must be answered. "Do drugs and alcohol, over a long period of time, help in solving problems, or do they create new problems, possibly more serious than the earlier problem they were used to solve?"

DRUGS AND ALCOHOL FOR INCREASING KNOWLEDGE ABOUT ONE'S SELF

A final use of drugs and alcohol is concerned with how these substances might aid us in better understanding our personal self. The use of drugs and alcohol for this purpose has been repeated by many people actually using various drugs and alcohol, and is not an easy question to answer. After all, what works for one person may not work for another. It is very hard to dispute or question what someone else has actually experienced under the influence of drugs or alcohol.

In thinking of how drugs and alcohol might create new forms of personal knowledge, it is important to remember one major fact about drugs and alcohol. *Neither drugs nor alcohol creates new patterns of nervous system activity.* In other words, whatever type of drug or alcohol used, it does not create or originate any form of knowledge or information you do not already possess.

What drugs and alcohol do when they appear to offer us new experiences or new pieces of knowledge is to alter or change our usual process of thinking. This change can occur in many ways, but basically drugs and alcohol act on how we perceive the environment around us. If a drug intensifies or heightens our visual or auditory senses, then we do indeed see and hear things differently. If, on the other hand, the drug mutes or dulls our visual or auditory powers, then this too affects what we normally see or hear.

Drugs also affect our memories. Under the influence of alcohol or drugs we may remember things we had long forgotten or memories may seem to change. If on the one hand we find our memories different through drugs or alcohol—and we add to this a new way of experiencing the environment—then certainly it appears that new information and knowledge can be gained from drugs and alcohol.

A question at this point often raised by persons against the use of drugs and alcohol goes something like this: "Aren't there other experiences far safer and more powerful than drugs and alcohol for gaining new forms of knowledge? What of hypnosis, psychotherapy, meditation, and other means of arriving at new personal awareness? Aren't these equally of use to you and less dangerous and harmful?"

This question must be considered by anyone seriously using drugs or alcohol as a major means of increasing her knowledge about herself. A final question for anyone using drugs for any reason is related to your survival as a member of society. The question is simply this: "*How does the drug or alcohol you use—especially if you use it over an extended period of time—affect your relationships with your friends, family, and society?*"

The answer to this question must be yours. No one else can answer it for you. It is an honest and serious question, and you might need additional help before you actually feel confident in your answer. The references and books that follow might be of help in deciding this question.

FURTHER READING

D. F. ABERLE. *The Peyote Religion Among the Navajo.* Chicago: Aldine, 1966. An anthropologist studies the use of peyote among the Navajo and how this drug is used in religious ritual.

W. BURROUGHS. *Speed.* New York: Olympia Press, 1970. The world of the speed freak as seen in a humorous portrayal of one young person on the move.

R. COLES. *The Grass Pipe.* Boston: Little, Brown, 1969. A novel about young teens and their early experiences in using marijuana by an outstanding psychiatrist.

W. J. CRADDOCK. *Be Not Content.* New York: Doubleday, 1970. A novel depicting the extensive drug culture in California at the height of the psychedelic revolution.

D. EBIN,ED. *Drug Experiences*. New York: Grove Press, 1965. First-person descriptions of writers, addicts, and professional people who have experienced the use of various drugs and chemical substances.

V. ELY. *Some of My Best Friends Were Addicts*. Old Tappan, N.J.: Revell Press, 1968. Accounts of the drug culture as seen through the eyes of a female sympathetic observer.

S. FIDDLE. *Portraits from a Shooting Gallery*. New York: Harper & Row, 1967. Stories and case studies of people caught up in the world of drugs.

R. GOLDSMITH. *The Poetry of Rock*. New York: Bantam Books, 1969. The effect of drugs through reprint of seventy folk and rock songs and a discussion of their impact on American society.

H. GREEN. *I Never Promised You a Rose Garden*. New York: Holt, Rinehart & Winston, 1964. A schizophrenic girl's struggle for sanity.

I. HOLLAND. *Heads You Win, Tails I Lose*. Philadelphia: J. Lippincott, 1973. Seeking popularity and relief from difficulties at home, a fat girl turns to amphetamines.

M. HYDE. *Alcohol: Drink or Drug*. New York: McGraw-Hill, 1974. The most up-to-date book directed toward high school students and their decisions about drinking.

M. E. KERR. *Dinky Hocker Shoots Smack*. New York: Harper & Row, 1972. A fat, unhappy girl grows plumper while her mother counsels drug addicts.

L. KINGMAN. *The Peter Pan Bag*. Boston: Houghton Mifflin, 1970. A seventeen year old young woman's summer spent in the Boston drug culture allows her to examine the meanings of freedom.

RUTGERS UNIVERSITY CENTER OF ALCOHOL STUDIES. *How Alcohol Affects the Body*. A pamphlet for high school students. *What the Body Does with Alcohol*. Companion pamphlet. Both available for 25 cents from the Center at Rutgers University, New Brunswick, New Jersey 08903.

L. M. SCHULMAN, ED. *The Loners: Short Stories About the Young Alienated*. New York: Macmillan, 1970. A collection of well-known short stories centered around the theme of alienation.

Spiritual Choices

Discovering Your Spirituality

JOYCE SLAYTON MITCHELL

Elizabeth Cady Stanton, organizer of the first Women's Rights Convention in Seneca Falls, New York, in 1848, wrote: "I do not believe that any man ever saw or talked with God. I do not believe that God inspired the Mosaic code, or told the historians what they say he did about women, for all the religions on the face of the earth degrade her, and so long as women accept the position that they assign her, her emancipation is impossible" (Woman's Bible, 1895).

As long as the top job in a church or synagogue cannot be held by a woman—solely on the basis of sex —then girls and women will get the message that they are not quite as close to God as men are. Institutions define roles. In the case of religion, women are told that they can prepare and serve the church supper but, in many churches, only men can serve communion, the Lord's supper. Leadership and decision-making jobs are open to women in most Protestant denominations, but a closer look shows that ordained women are in the rural or inner-city churches where no one else will go. There is a direct correlation between the low budget of the church and the jobs open to a woman pastor.

Because religious institutions are man-centered rather than God-centered, many young women forget the whole thing and deny their own spirituality. This chap-

ter deals with the idea that women are spiritual beings whether we choose to do anything religious about it or not. We are spiritual beings with the potential for wholeness when we integrate everything about ourselves. Not merely the obvious or what we talk about or what our society says is what we are.

Becoming a person isn't easy. Becoming altogether is often a struggle against someone putting us in a clearcut category, in a box. With that box goes a label, and with the label go all the particular personality traits that fit the name on the label. People are grouped into male or female, black or white, young or old, rich or poor, worldly or spiritual. People in a category are are treated alike—regardless of the "I." And people in one box or category often turn against their opposite number on the scale. As a result, female against male becomes sexism, black against white becomes racism, young against old becomes ageism, and humanity against spirituality becomes secularism.

Not only are these opposites to be found in groups of people, but there are differences *within* us that we must recognize and accept before we can become an integrated person. Or if we cannot accept our differences, we can at least be aware of what we are like and work at accepting the inconsistencies. Becoming integrated is always an ongoing process.

To understand what we are like we must learn that our wholeness includes both female and male, both young and old, both human and spiritual. Barbara Krasner, a leading family therapist, writes in her chapter on Judaism, that "every man and every woman has a special blend of both sets of [male and female] characteristics; that each human being has the ability to be active *and* passive, assertive and submissive, logical and illogical, aggressive and retiring, intellectual and emotional, hard and soft, just and forgiving." And we read in Lyn Wark's chapter describing Christianity that just as our human relationships must grow, so too must our spiritual relationship mature if we are to have a meaningful life. To be whole means to include everything we experience about ourselves—not merely the obvious or what we talk about or what our society says is what we are.

Society tells girls and women that they are passive, submissive, and illogical. When a girl discovers that she is active, assertive, and logical, she often goes through stages of thinking that there is something wrong with her. She thinks that what she sees in herself can't be true, that other people in her group aren't like she is—she doesn't fit the label on the box. She isn't what "girls" are like or what "young" is like or what "white" is like. And if she has learned from our religious institutions and their denial of equality for women in religious leadership and decision making that women aren't quite as close to God as men are, then she will never know what "spirituality" is.

Women in the women's movement are working to help women know and accept everything about themselves. To know and to accept our human condition is to accept our sexuality, to accept that we are starting young and getting old, and to accept our spirituality in spite of the sexism in religious institutions. We are indeed spiritual beings, just as we are sexual beings, intellectual beings, aging beings, and social beings.

We are going beyond religious institutions and their traditional white male theology to seek our own concepts of spirituality. Our concept of spirituality will relate God to us as a female. Our Western culture's religious tradition has put God in the position of the grand patriarch, writes the Reverend Patricia Budd Kepler of Harvard Divinity School. "We have made God the prime model for the white male oppressor, the model for all oppressors." But, she says, "there is another vision of God." "There is a God who is feminine and masculine so that I, like my brother, can know I am in the image of God as a woman; that as She is complete, I am complete, all right as a woman." Beyond our cultural God "is the real God who wants to be loved as God loves, to be forgiven as God forgives, to be human and spiritual, to touch and be touched, to move and be moved, to be passive and at peace, as well as active and in struggle." Continues the Reverend Ms. Kepler, "God wants to end the alienation between divinity and humanity, between maleness and femaleness."

Recognizing and accepting our spirituality isn't only for women who have a Judeo-Christian background. It is also for you who have learned your religion through the teachings of Hinduism, Buddhism, or Islam, and for you who have been turned off from your childhood religion or have been brought up without religion and never noticed that you are a spiritual being. Many women who have not been concerned with getting beyond themselves in a spiritual sense are young women who have been busy finding themselves in the first place. Finding what you can do in school, who your friends are, and getting along with everybody with whom you want to get along is often enough to do.

It is at this point of finding some things out about yourself, of who you are and what you can do, that you can even be free enough to notice where the system is leading you. Many educators treat students as if they are a commodity. School years are organized into an economic investment concept, so that your curriculum and college decisions will lead you to the "big job"—if you are a boy—and to a wife who buys commodities—if you are a girl.

When you start to see that getting everything our materialistic society has in store for you—dates, member of school clubs, summer trips, clothes, cosmetics, car and allowance—isn't enough, you may begin to whisper to yourself, "Is this all there is? Is this what getting those dreams is all about?"

When the physical and human possibilities become a reality, then we look at what we're like and ask, What else is there? What are my possibilities? What can I be? Who is the woman I can become? What *is* my nature? It is now that we turn toward our spiritual possibilities. The last thing. After we have tried becoming a person only on a human level and on our own secular terms and seen it and found it and bought it and said—this is *all* there is! We finally learn that we CANNOT live an abundant life with others—one with love, and joy, and kindness and gentleness, and mercy, and faithfulness, and within grace—by bread alone!

A Christian Choice

M. LYNETTE WARK

Lyn Wark, a physician in Sydney, Australia, and a former medical missionary in New Guinea sees the connection between her commitment to Christ and the rest of life. She understands the integrated person. She uses Scripture to tell us about Christianity—about Jesus Christ, "the image of the invisible God" (Colossians 1:15).[1]

Jesus made a unique contribution to the setting free of roles for women by going directly against His culture to treat them, as he treated all people—with equality. He chose a woman to witness that He was the Messiah at a time when Judaic law didn't allow women to bear legal witness. Again, a woman first witnessed His resurrection. Jesus countered the only acceptable role for women as childbearers and housekeepers. When a woman blessed His mother for giving birth, He replied, "Blessed rather, are those who hear the Word of God and keep it!" (Luke 11:28); and when Martha asked if Mary should help with the cooking, Jesus replied that Mary had discovered learning about God, the only thing worth being concerned about (Luke 10:42).

Jesus taught that one must be born again, in a

---

[1] Scripture quotations are from the Revised Standard Version.

spiritual sense, in order to have a personal relationship with God (John 3:3). When you make a commitment to Christ, you have a new life, you are a new creation in which you can grow toward your completeness. This life integrates all the human qualities within you; it is spiritual and eternal. This life responds to a God who is complete. The new creation frees male and female roles so that the gifts of each can be used for the glory of God. A commitment to Christ is a commitment to a life that brings together differences in people, and differences within people, a life where "there is neither Jew nor Greek, there is neither slave nor free, there is neither male nor female; for you are all one in Christ Jesus" (Galatians 3:28).

WHO HE WAS

Jesus Christ was born almost two thousand years ago in Palestine. Before His birth His mother was visited by an angel who said, "And behold, you will conceive in your womb and bear a son, you shall call His name Jesus. He will be great, and will be called the Son of the Most High" (Luke 1:31–32). His birth fulfilled God's message through His prophets (Matthew 1:22). At the time of His birth the landscape shone bright with the glory of the Lord, and the angel announced, "For to you is born this day in the city of David a Savior, who is Christ the Lord" (Luke 2:11).

HOW HE LIVED

Jesus lived lovingly. He lived within the love of God and asked others to live within His love (John 15:9). He met everyone's needs in a very personal way. The Scriptures tell of His miracles that enabled Him to speak and make the blind see, the deaf hear, and the lame walk.

Sex, age, money, status, nationality, and all the

human measurements of people made no difference in His loving attitude toward them, nor to His challenge to reach each person He ever met to teach them about the possibility of their own personal relationship with God. The possibility to be a new creation.

Jesus wanted us to learn that the two most important Commandments were to love God and to love our neighbors as ourselves (Matthew 22:38–39). About these Commandments He told us to keep these and we would find that we are obeying all the others. This message was spoken to everyone: to women, to the poor, to the politically alienated, to criminals, to the sick, and to men in power. Social scientists tell us now that when any group of people are not given equal access to responsibility and leadership within their own communities they learn to feel second-rate and unworthy of loving. Jesus Christ understood oppression nearly two thousand years ago and he knew that he *had* to make a special point about women and all oppressed people to bring them into personhood (self-love) before loving others (giving) could be a possibility.

"A study of the Gospels reveals that there is no doubt that Jesus was making an obvious, special point about the worth and equality of women and men; partly because He loved people, but more importantly, because He understood the far-reaching and damaging effects for both women and men, when men assert their authority over women. Jesus understood the effect of oppression of one group over another and that is the reason He confronted the prejudices between men and women so boldly throughout His ministry." So writes the Reverend Mary Cline Detrick in her sermon delivered at the Annual Conference of the Church of the Brethren.

Christ was as concerned about teaching a woman— a nameless, lonely, and alienated Samaritan He met in a chance encounter—as he was concerned with teaching the important Jewish religious leader Nicodemus (John 13). His purpose was to bring to everyone the

Good News of the Kingdom of God. The Kingdom of God (the person-God relationship) is within us, taught Jesus. He spent his ministry asking people to believe in God and to obey His Commandments so that this relationship would grow.

He used stories, miracles, descriptions, proverbs, and parables to teach about God and His Commandments for a life with Him. Jesus continually broke cultural tradition in order to treat all kinds of people (second-class citizens oppressed within their society) as worthy persons who could love God. Even though a male Jew never spoke to a woman in public, or to a person from Samaria, it was a Samaritan woman—at the village well—who was asked to be the first witness to others that Jesus was the Messiah, God's anointed One (John 4:26).

At another time He broke with the custom of His time to question the law that said only the woman is to be punished for adultery. The law was clear. It was based on the Old Testament assumption that it is woman who tempts man, that woman was the origin of sin. A woman must be stoned to death if guilty of adultery.

It happened one day when a woman was hustled along a narrow street by angry men. She knew they were hypocrites, but she also knew the law and was frightened. The group found Jesus, stood before Him, and one man cried out, "She ought to die, our law says she should be stoned to death, because we caught her in the act of adultery." Jesus stayed where He was. He looked at no one. Presently, in a silence that was profound, He started writing in the dust on the ground. Then He spoke slowly, "Let him who is without sin among you be the first to throw a stone at her." One by one, those hypocritical accusers stole away. He raised His head. "Where are your accusers?" He asked. "Gone," she answered. "Neither do I condemn you" came His reply. "Go, and do not sin again" (John 8:1–11). Jesus illustrated that men and women are both responsible for their actions—men can no longer blame their sins on women. Women, too, have the possibility for a new life with God.

When Jesus healed people He gave them more than a physical cure. At the time when Jesus healed a woman bent over for eighteen years, His disciples were not surprised at the healing but were surprised to hear him refer to her as the "daughter of Abraham" (Luke 13:10–17). Reverend Mary Detrick explains that in the Jewish tradition only men of great faith were called "sons of Abraham." But Jesus implied that women, too, could have a direct connection to Abraham, the father of their faith. When Jesus called the bent woman "daughter of Abraham" he broadened the Old Testament covenant with God to include all women to stand unapologetically, with dignity, as full-fledged daughters of God. In Christianity, baptism for all persons, not circumcision for males, is the sign of a covenantal relationship with God.

Christ's loving way with other people is an example for us in our lives. But His message is more than His way with people. He came to bring the good news about God, about a spiritual life of our own with God. Our chance to be a new creation. Paul writes, "Therefore, if anyone is in Christ, [s/he] is a new creation; the old has passed away, behold, the new has come" (II Corinthians 5:17). About this new creation, Jesus said:

"My teaching is not mine, but His who sent me." *John 7:16*

"I am the Bread of Life; [s/he] who comes to me shall not hunger, and [s/he] who believes in me shall never thirst." *John 6:35*

"I am the Light of the world: [s/he] who follows me will not walk in darkness, but will have the light of life." *John 8:12*

"A new commandment I give to you, that you love one another; even as I have loved you, that you also love one another. By this all people will know that you are my disciples, if you have love for one another." *John 13:34–35*

HOW HE DIED

During the three years that Jesus was in His public ministry, the tensions mounted between Him and those who saw Him as a threat to their authority. They said, "By our laws He ought to die because he has made Himself the Son of God" (John 19:7).

He was condemned to death by crucifixion and after death His body was sealed in a cave. On the third day after his death, His tomb was found empty, and He was seen by many of His friends and followers. For forty days He walked, talked, and ate with His disciples and friends. Some found it hard to believe that He was really with them. One close friend, Thomas, declared he wouldn't believe that the disciples had seen their Lord unless Jesus physically proved it. Jesus came to him and told him to touch His crucifixion wounds and said, "Stop doubting and believe!" When Jesus proved his presence he told Thomas, "Have you believed because you have seen me? Blessed are those who haven't seen me and yet believe" (John 20:26–29).

Christ's death wakes us up; with Him we are resurrected into a new way of relating to other people. All the prejudices which used to matter fall away when we are a new creation.

We are called to this new creation so that we can change our views of each other. We are called to love one another so much that we are different people— not just a little bit changed, here and there, but to be transformed in our relationships with others, writes Mary Detrick. Paul says that being in tune with Christ is what transforms us.

"Jesus balanced the scales on the nature of God," continues Ms. Detrick. "God exemplifies that being which is powerful and caring; almighty and protector; unchanging, yet forgiving; judge and lover." That nature of God is a complete nature. The nature of God includes male and female.

WHO HE IS

Two thousand years ago Jesus rose from the dead and His spirit is alive today in everyone who accepts Him and believes in Him. His life is our way to God, His death is our way to our new creation, His rising again is our proof that we too can live a spiritual and eternal life. He is the Way, the Truth, and the new life.

Jesus Christ is Lord.

A Jewish Choice

BARBARA KRASNER

Barbara Krasner, a family therapist at the Eastern Pennsylvania Psychiatric Institute in Philadelphia, is an activist in the human rights movement and a Ph.D. candidate in religion. Her interest in Judaism for girls is expressed in this unique chapter where she urges girls and women to contend with God within Judaism. She writes that Israel means "one who contends with God," and she continues, "to contend with God means to discover God." Even though Judaism has traditionally focused on the relationship between God and men, Ms. Krasner believes that girls and women can find their own way to discover God, to witness to Creation.

She writes, "Hidden in musty books and unturned pages, there is testimony to an unresolved struggle in Judaism—centered around sexuality. Its roots run deep. Its dimensions bear study. It has to do with women and their right to study Torah."

DATELINE JERUSALEM. The Western Wall of Solomon's Temple: Birds fly over the Wall, pigeons nest in it, green plants grow out of it. People pray at it and tuck messages between the crevices of its stones. And the stones answer back. They tell a different story to every passerby.

The Wall is Judaism's most hallowed place. For Jews it is a symbol of the past and of the present. It is a symbol and a promise of the future world to come. It conveys a history. It extends a choice. It speaks of life and death, of peace and war, of hope and fear, of love and violence, of joy and pain. Beneath its towering heights Jews dance and sing, laugh and cry, touch and sway. Within its mystical circle their feet rest on holy ground. Here they belong, outsiders no more.

Outsiders no more! The sentence resounds. But it's not yet a fact. For exclusion comes in many forms. Denial exists in many shapes. People are wounded in many ways. Exile has personal dimensions as well as national dimensions. One can be a wandering Jew within the body of the People Israel (all Jews everywhere) as well as within the framework of hostile nations.

Beneath the Wall there is a courtyard. On Friday night people gather there in anticipation of the beginning of the Sabbath. They are waiting to greet the "Sabbath Queen"—the "heavenly" (Godly) sign of peace on earth.

In synagogues around the world the Queen or Bride endures through song:

> Come, let us go to meet the Sabbath,
> for it is a source of blessing. From
> the very beginning it was ordained;
> last in creation, first in God's plan.
> Come, my friend, to meet the bride;
> let us welcome the Sabbath.
> —Daily Prayer Book

But here at the Wall the Queen is personified:

A pious man, clothed in white garments that connote purity, appears from the midst of the crowd. His arrival is a signal. Melody fills the air. Prayer rises aloft with all the power that human intention can muster. It has happened again. The work week has ended.

The time has come to raise the dream of peace to

human consciousness: to recognize it and to live it in such a way that the dream can be made real. "Not only the hands of a [person] celebrate the day, the tongue and the soul keep the Sabbath" (A. J. Heschel). The time has come to practice peace so that, reminded of what it is like, we can bring it back to the every day world with freshness and renewed strength.

That way, through the persistent efforts of its inhabitants, the whole world will know peace one day (Zech. 14:8, 9). Until that time we need to learn how to pursue peace. We need to imagine how it will feel.

But now, at the Wall, something is wrong. The singing, the swaying, the body language that indicates rapture and inclusion, is limited to one side of the Wall —the side on which the men stand. On the other side of the *mehitzah* (barrier) the women pray too, but silently and passively. They show no joy. Some are weeping.

Occasionally one of them glances toward the men. She is not caught up, as they are, in ritual celebration of life. For the most part she is an observer. Present for the purpose of corporate prayer, in the deepest sense she prays alone—outside the pale of communal expectation, unbound by the invisible yoke of internal obligation. She is cut off from the main actors in God's drama. Or so she may think.

She may have taken on the ways of her mother without reflecting on the world of her daughter. Mindful only of the religious practice of her family or of her particular religious community or synagogue, she may have begun to act by rote. Accepting a "place" that is assigned her, by direction or innuendo, she may have begun to be hooked by a habit.

If she's forgotten to press for answers, she may eventually forget how to question. She may be ignoring the options before her. She may be sledding along the surface of the layers of possibility. By confining the fire of her spirit to a feeling of comfort and safety, she may be an accomplice in making Jewish life dead and stale.

In any case she cannot proceed uncritically. She must regard her own life thoughtfully. For she is a link in the chain of tradition. As a daughter of Sarah and of Abraham, she must walk uncertainly, but in trust—expecting to be guided through distant and uncharted lands, staying open to unanticipated blessings.

She must retain personal responsibility for making choices (Deut. 30:19). She must affirm the uniqueness of her own specific body, mind, and spirit. She cannot permit others to affect her life by determining her values, by defining her role, and by deciding her religious behavior *without her insights and input*. She must resist placing her future into the hands of those who may not know her needs.

Should she silently submit to the dictates of unreasoning fiats and formulas imposed upon her without consideration for the longings of her soul, she would lose touch with the dictates of her own conscience. She would be denying the importance of her own existence. She would be forgetting the Hasidic (pious) tale that affirms that each human being has two pockets full of understanding: in the one it is written that from dust she comes and to dust she must return; in the other it is written that the world is made for her and her alone. She must take understanding, first from one pocket and then from another, as her life requires.

A mature and balanced perspective requires both humility and the right of every person to be heard. No one can speak in the place of another. No one can live vicariously through another. Each must listen for God's Word as it addresses her special situation. Torah belongs to women as it belongs to every Jew.

Each person must remember that Torah (written and oral instruction) is timeless and speaks anew to every generation. She must recall that within the soil of Torah the seeds of Wisdom (Proverbs 8) lie fallow —waiting to be cultivated, waiting to be brought to flower with ever clearer and richer meaning. She must be reminded that all personal and communal deepening takes place on the narrow ridge that stretches between the two poles of rootedness and change.

Jewish women are faced with a *mehitzah* at the Wall of the Temple. They are faced with literal and figurative barriers in synagogues around the world. But the most dangerous *mehitzah* of all is the *mehitzah* of the mind. It may be overcome and transcended when women reach out over time and space; when they permit their memory to recollect important events and affirmations in Jewish history, and to help to record them in the hearts and in the psyches of their own generation.

At the outset women can begin by comprehending that Judaism has a broad and flexible framework in which a variety of views and postures flourish side by side. In ages past as in the present, it has had many forms and foci. Perceiving Judaism through their own set of spectacles, people have called it by many names. Israel has been known as a People and as an ethical force, as a nation-state and as a historical tradition, as a lodestone of culture and as a paradigm of civilization.

At one time or another Israel has been any or all these things. But her truest calling is in her name. For Israel means "one who contends with God." The underlying thread of continuity that binds generations of Jews—black and white, male and female, East and West, ingathered and dispersed—to each other has been a common recognition of the Lord of Israel and a readiness to contend with Him.

> To contend with God means to seek out our own Truth and to establish a living relationship to it; and then to live that Truth wherever life carries us.

> To contend with God means to stand our ground at the same time that we are learning how to listen obediently and to imagine another's side.

To contend with God means to understand Reciprocity as the central obligation in all relationships.

To contend with God means to learn to say "I" as He does—in love (E. Wiesel). It means to recognize that in Judaism the two primary attributes of God are compassion (*rachamim*) and justice (*din*)—attributes that all human beings are called to imitate.

To contend with God means to be in a deepening and more faithful relationship to ourselves, to each other, and to the Eternal Thou. It means that not only must we study Torah, we must strive to be Torah.

To contend with God means getting your head together, that is, having an undivided will and living a life of intended integrity; and at some point during the course of that life, discovering the Rainbow Sign (God; Gen. 9:12–17).

To contend with God means to realize that the Lord of Israel cares for all of His creatures. It means to learn that "the Holy Spirit may rest upon Gentiles and Jews, upon man and woman, upon man-servant and maid-servant, depending solely upon the human deed" (*Seder Eliyahu Rabba IX*).

To contend with God means to understand the interlocking nature of the individual and the People, of the People and the Land, of the Land and the world, and of the world and the Living God.

To contend with God means to sense that He is not far off but close at hand (Jer. 23:23, 24). It means to learn to intuit His voice, to accept His discipline, to be responsive to His call (Jer. 7:27, 28).

To contend with God means to renew Israel's convenant with Him—through ourselves, in our own time, out of the process of our own growth and yearning, out of the experience of our own seeking and finding (Amos 5:4).

To contend with God means to perceive that real wealth is to be found neither in abstract scholarship nor in material goods, but in the practice of love, justice, and righteousness in the earth (Jer. 9:23, 24).

To contend with God means to wrestle with life from exactly where we are. It means to be ourselves. It means to refuse to compromise by pretending to be what we're not, or by conforming to the standards of others. It means that we must heed the Hasidic tale that says, "If I am I because you are you, and you are you because I am. I, then I am not I and you are not .you. But if you are you because you are you, and I am I because I am I, then you are really you and I am really I."

To contend with God means to reaffirm that Judaism's supreme value is unity. That is, when we recite the Shema (Deut. 6:4–9) daily, we are citing God's norm for behavior and His call for repairing existence. We are speaking of wholeness and healing and harmony. We are declaring that all matters are interconnected. We are asserting that beneath all separation there is human solidarity, that beyond what meets the eye there is a Secret Ground.

To contend with God means to remember His imagelessness. It means to recall that He possesses no physical attributes, no marks of gender. He is to be compared to neither man nor woman.

To contend with God means to bear the awareness that when we call Him "He," it is because of language and grammar. It is a misinformed way of thinking impressed on us early in childhood. To conceive of God as male is to encourage a faulty habit.

To contend with God means to be mindful that, when we pray to our Father in Heaven, He is not our male progenitor (Patai). Instead we're expressing a feeling of dependence and reliance. We are talking to a Parent, to a Being Who's greater than we are.

To contend with God means to absorb the fact that during the course of thousands of years others have walked where we walk and hurt as we hurt and struggled as we struggle. The issues may have differed but the process was the same.

Some Jews were destroyed for wanting to determine the values and the conditions for living their own lives. Some were derided and taunted. Some surrendered to the difficulty of the task of standing their ground and to the pressure of their own pain. And some contended and survived and endured and changed the fact of existence.

Some contending is cataclysmic and bloody. Other contending is quiet and persistent. Some victories are won by gunfire and revolution. Other victories are won by resolution and evolution; they emerge from an idea that has met its time, from a moment that's pregnant with promise.

An idea whose time has come does not spring forth of its own accord. It is drawn from the past, encountered in the present, and conveyed to the future. There are no proofs for its validity. There are only witnesses. Its bearers are those to whose minds and hearts it speaks. It finds justification in its life-giving qualities. It cannot be argued. It can only be lived.

That man and woman are equally created and endowed and therefore equally responsible and obligated in the realm of religion as elsewhere is an idea whose time has come. It is a reality increasingly drawn from empirical evidence. It is conceptually supported by the notion of androgyny.

Androgyny means that within each human being there are bisexual qualities. Within each one of us there exists a unique balance of masculine and feminine characteristics. Androgyny means that within our psyches there exist active and passive tendencies which serve to inform us and to shape us.

Androgyny runs counter to the claim that men are "naturally" active, assertive, logical, aggressive, intellectual, hard, and inclined to demand justice while women are "naturally" passive, submissive, illogical, retiring, emotional, soft, and inclined to forgiveness. It suggests, instead, that conditioned by our genes, our training, our environment, and the patterns of our families, these qualities exist in tandem within every person.

The notion of androgyny suggests that every man and every woman has a special blend of both sets of characteristics; that each human being has the ability to be active *and* passive, assertive and submissive, logical and illogical, aggressive and retiring, intellectual and emotional, hard and soft, just and forgiving.

Therefore the life that a person leads is determined by her own internal balance of "masculine" and "feminine" qualities, and by the relationships with others that her personal predisposition allows. Her possibilities for maturation and role options are not finally locked into a "prison of gender" (C. Heilbrun). She is not determined by her physical form and its functions. Her body is her home in the universe. She can be comfortable in it and grow in it and give life through it. But she is not finally limited by it except through death.

The notion of androgyny is drawn from many sources in many cultures. It is to be found in the first chapter of Genesis, commented upon in the Midrash, expanded in Jewish legend, indicated in the Zohar, developed by Jewish thinkers, picked up by Sigmund Freud, and enlarged by Carl Jung.

Androgyny, from a Jewish perspective, is based on the understanding that God is a revealing God who stays in touch with human beings. That way people know about Him and what He wills for the world. Though we have never learned Who God is, we know that He is, and that from time to time—on rare occasions—He makes Himself known to His creatures through the process of revelation.

One of the things that God has revealed is that human being is a reflection of Divine Being: "And God said, Let Us make man in Our image, after Our likeness." . . . "Male and female created He them" (Gen. 1:26, 27). It is written that Adam, God's first representative on earth, was made in the Divine image.

In Jewish thought the basis for androgyny is the sexual structure inherent in all being. Created after the image of God, man and woman exist. Part of their existence is determined by sex. Man and woman exist as sexual beings. To be a sexual being is to have a capacity for sexual relationship. The sex act is part of human sexuality. But human sexuality goes beyond the sex act. "The words 'male and female He created them' make known the high dignity of man. They teach us that every figure which does not comprise male and female elements is not a true and proper figure. . . ." (The Zohar I).

Qualities as well as action are a part of human sexuality. Heaven is wedded to earth. And man "unites both heavenly and earthly qualities within himself" (L. Ginzberg). Every human being has "two faces." It is said that the first human being had "two faces" which Adam bore alone. But Adam was lonely and overburdened and complained to God Who took pity on him in his isolation. God gave Adam a companion whom He cloned from the original person. "The creation of woman from man was possible because Adam originally had two faces which were separated at the birth of Eve" (*The Legends of the Jews,* tr. by H. Szold). After Eve was created, Adam abandoned his original name: now "Adam called his wife *Ishah* (Woman) and himself he called *Ish* (Man)" (L. Ginzberg).

Sacred legend in Jewish literature, rooted in Scripture and in rabbinic commentary on Scripture, uncovers a model of man, who created in the image of God, is androgynous in kind. Transformed from "his" original condition, Adam becomes *Ish* and *Ishah*—changing his name to commemorate his individuation, and incorporating God's Name in the names of man and woman to shield them against all harm (L. Ginzberg).

Here human wholeness is perceived in an androgynous ideal. But people mature to "completion" not only through their inner world but also in the world of relationship. The original human being "was the only one who was created by the hand of God" (L. Ginzberg). When Adam was separated, God expressed concern that the relationship of man and woman to each other and to Him be maintained. So when, by Divine resolution, Adam became a man and woman, they were rejoined in a new way.

"The wedding of the first couple was celebrated with pomp never repeated in the whole course of human history since. God Himself, before presenting her to Adam, attired and adorned Eve as a bride" (L. Ginzberg). Reunited, man and woman again become Adam who, in the beginning, lived in harmony and knew that God is One. About them God said, "They are more pleasing in My sight than the sacrifices Israel will offer upon the altar" (L. Ginzberg).

Streaming powerfully through one current of Jewish thought is a message whose time may well have come: "And God said, Let Us make man in Our image, after Our likeness." . . . "Male and female created He them" (The Holy Scriptures). Man and woman—equally created, equally endowed, equally pleasing in the sight of God in all their vast multiplicity. Man and woman—equally balanced, equally obligated, equally responsible for the quality of human life in all its great variety.

Between them they carry the promise of Creation. They are more precious than any ritual. The wholeness embodied in them and the Oneness carried through them may one day suffice to repair the injured order of existence.

The promise is in the offing. But the force of inertia remains. To overcome that force women must over-

come disinterest and despair, indifference and illiteracy
—on their own part and on the part of men. Awkward
or angry, they must probe the possibilities and ferret
out direction. They must counter the weight of Jewish
history that has thudded down on the side of men.

In the sphere of corporate religious practice, scholarship, and leadership, a message has been conveyed:
No women need apply. In the main, men have par-
ticipated in delivering that message, offering weak and
tired answers to women who wondered why. In the
main, women have received the message and accepted
it without a challenge. Their behavior has been collu-
sive. The burden of responsibility rests in both directions.

Together they have shaped and misshaped religious
life—in the family and in the community. Together
they have created an imbalance whose impact has
gathered force over the centuries. Together they have
ignored the instruction of their own literature.

Hidden in musty books and unturned pages, there is
testimony to an unresolved struggle in Judaism—centered around sexuality. Its roots run deep. Its dimensions bear study. It has to do with women and their
right to study Torah. History, unheeded, repeats its
message. But not all men conveyed the same message.
And not all women accepted it. A small band of people
opposed the tide.

The Talmud mentions Beruria, a second-century
scholar who was learned in *halacha* (law) and Scripture; and Michal, "daughter of the Cushite," who work
prayer straps (*tefillin*) with the sages protesting; and
female Pharisees who gave themselves up to prayer and
fasting. It reports that Rabbi Johanan argued against
the time-worn assertion that women are the cause of
sin, citing cases in point; and that Ben Azzai declared
that a man is under obligation to teach his daughter
Torah.

A woman is cited as experiencing revelation in the
days of Moses: "What an ordinary maidservant saw at

the crossing of the Sea was not seen by Isaiah, Ezekiel, and all the Prophets" (Mekilta Shirata).

The Zohar, a thirteenth-century mystical work with roots, some say, in antiquity, cites Sarah as the proto-type for Jewish women: Sarah to whom alone of all the women of Scripture a whole section of the Torah is devoted; Sarah who "never attached herself to the serpent"; Sarah who reached a profound level of personal piety; Sarah who maintained eternal life for herself, her husband, and all her descendants after her (The Zohar II).

The Hasidic movement, initiated in Eastern Europe in the middle of the eighteenth century by the Baal Shem Tov (Master of the Good Name), signaled a renewal of Jewish life. Marked by fervor and song, by joy and service, by prayer and intention, Hasidim—people who are faithful to God—poured old wine into new wineskins. And they drank from the depths of the Jewish Soul.

Among them were women, some say, who possessed the Holy Spirit. We learn of Adel (Odel), daughter of the *Besht*: Feige, his granddaughter; Frieda, daughter of Israel of Kozienice; Sarah, daughter of Joshua Heschel Teumim Frankel; Malkele the Triskerun; and Hannah Rachel, the "Maid of Ludmir."

And now again, linked by a chain that encircles the world, a movement has begun that may signal renewal in Jewish life: Jews are reclaiming for their own the basic right and obligation of every human being. In all the complexity of modern times, they want to determine their own values and to define their own identities. Overcoming centuries of wandering, some have turned to the Land and made the desert bloom. Others are plowing the arid soil of human hearts, planting seeds of spirit there. Among them are women.

Again many currents converge, drawn from an Ocean that will not be stilled. Here a woman gathers courage and penetrates the Talmud. And she becomes a scholar. There a woman marries *and* goes on to study to become a rabbi.

Here a youngster braves a teacher and wears a skull-cap, now for her a symbol, a token of defiance in the face of bigness and unredeemed tradition. There one makes *havdalah* (the ceremony that closes the Sabbath), supported by her family, but uncertain of their friends.

Here a woman hears her children asking, and takes on the yoke of *kashruth* (food laws). There a young girl learns the Torah, instructed by her father and encouraged by his love.

In the Negev a young woman rejoices, wrapped in the mystery of Sabbath. She is affronted by a *mehitzah*. But she is lured by the magic of song. She has found her Place in the desert. But still she is not quite at home.

In a major American city, a girl becomes a *bat mitzvah* (a service marking the ritual incorporation of a young woman into adulthood) in the basement of a church. She has been barred from reading from Torah in the synagogue where she was trained. One rabbi lends her a Torah. Another flies in from Jerusalem— to affirm her choice and direction, to receive her as an adult.

DATELINE JERUSALEM. The Western Wall of Solomon's Temple: Birds still fly over the Wall, pigeons nest in it, plants grow out of it. People pray at it and tuck messages between the crevices of its stones. And the stones answer back. They tell a different story to every passerby.

One young woman hangs back from the Wall. She has seen its stones and she loves them. And she has sent them a message. The stones have replied. They have told her her own special story: She may not approach them. She cannot pray there now.

She would demean the stones if she came to them in her present frame of being—with so many tears, and with so much aloneness and pain. She would make them less joyful. She would make them cry too. She must come to them as a person, bringing with her all of her wholeness. For Wholeness calls to wholeness. It can be no other way.

But the *mehitzah* will not permit it. It reduces her power of intention. It dampens the fire of her spirit. It makes her feel less than a person. It pollutes the gift of her heart.

So for now she must wait. She must find another way to witness to Creation, another place to be a bearer of her light.

She need not despair. For if she watches and listens, she will see and hear and learn that across light years Creation has endured, slowly yielding its secrets in time and space, in books and stories, in songs and symbols, in science and logic, in process and event. Chaos has been resisted and Night withstood, if not explained. And again and again, despite diversions and frailty, human kind has proved pliant and malleable.

It will happen again. It is happening now. One day she will stand before the Wall and all it implies. She will pray—wholeness seeking out Oneness. She will stand there as a person. And she will know that she has lived her own story and not another's. Through the instrument of her own life and not another's she will have witnessed to Creation—as a bearer of the Light.

Educational Choices

In High School

Study Is for Learning

JOYCE SLAYTON MITCHELL

Girls are often said to do better in school than boys because they study harder, are more conscientious about getting the right assignment, getting the work in on time, and doing work that is clear enough to read. It is said that girls want to please the teachers and authorities more, are more adaptable to the educational system, and therefore come out with better results. These remarks are usually made as if good study habits were a put-down for young women. Don't believe it! All serious students wish they had good study habits.

If you don't fit the description above and you need some help with your study habits, here are some things you may want to try. First, in order for you to make improvements, you must define study as your work. And as work that counts—give it top priority. Studying isn't just something everyone who goes to school has to do; its your job, your way to discover and learn about the world. Next, as soon as studying becomes more to you than "homework," you will see it as a worthwhile skill. Not because you want to get along within the system, but because it's your way to making your contribution to understanding the world.

Studying is work, *your* work. It is hard work and it must be done alone. Your mother and father have their daily work, long-term jobs, routine jobs, things they like and things they don't like about their work. You can expect the same from your schoolwork. Studying isn't natural. It may look like it's easy for others to study because they are some kind of "study creature" —but study is learned behavior and everyone who is a good worker has learned it. The sooner you realize that studying is not something extra, the sooner you realize the need for the skill. Hopefully you will then begin to get enjoyment out of the real reason for study —learning.

Many teachers, educators, and parents promote the idea that the classroom is the heart of learning. Studying then becomes doing something for the teacher or cramming for tests and examinations. In fact, the classroom situation is only your guide for what to study; your evaluation of how you do; your suggestions for new ways to look at materials such as tests, related readings, papers and projects about the particular subject.

In order to look at studying as something that has to do with *you,* you should understand that studying is for learning. And learning is what high school is all about. It is learning what you can do academically, what you can understand, how you can relate to new materials, what you can think about.

In order to get anything out of studying you must define it in such a way that it is important to you. You must set it up in your mind so that it counts. It has to have a top priority if it is going to work. If you can define your study time as your work, and that you must work nights, it will help. There is no question about the difficulty of the hour, especially if your parents are home from their work and watching TV or playing bridge or having late cocktails and dinner while you work—but your schedule is different. You have sports and clubs and time off for activities after school while your parents and most adults are still on their jobs.

At any rate, it won't come out fair or equal with adults because high school students who study on a regular, responsible basis *do* work more than adults who have a nine-to-five job. Your work schedule compares more readily with professional people in teaching, research, law, and medicine, or with business executives who work all hours. There is no doubt that a high school student who studies three hours a night works more than the forty-hour week! And three hours a night is about average for an *A* or *B* student with five academic subjects in a competitive high school.

As you work out your study schedule and find what you can do in terms of working alone, at the library, or with homework assignments, you will be learning what you can do in college, what you can do in your career after college. All your high school experiences are teaching you about your abilities and your interests. Studying is a key place for you to learn about your self-starting ability, your motivation, your persistence, your follow-through, and your ability to stick with a problem. These traits will build. You will learn all kinds of things that you can do as well as all kinds of things you *cannot* do because of your lack of good study skills.

Your ability to study will improve as the years pass. Self-discipline is a growing ability. Good study skills grow slowly. It takes time to learn to use your mind efficiently to understand all kinds of subjects, to memorize facts, to grasp new ideas, and to see relationships between the subjects you study and you and the world. If there is no way for you and study skills, then you should know that, for you, there is no way for you and college, or at least a liberal arts or competitive college.

HOW CAN YOU STUDY TO LEARN?

Many things will help you to study. Good teachers and interested parents who encourage you and work with you as you develop your study skills are the most help. But good teachers and interested parents are hard to find, and lucky is the student who has either! If you ask for help with your studying, from your homeroom teacher or your guidance counselor or one of the administrators, you should be able to find some-one who will encourage you so that your work will be something you look forward to.

If your family is working against you with distract-ing offers of other things to do and with noise in the house, you may be able to go to the local library, or to study as much as possible in school or after school, in place of sports or music or clubs. Some students do all their studying before they go home because they know that conditions at home don't work for study! These students get their work done right after school, in place of extracurricular school activities. They spend their time off with their families at night.

There are many books written about how to study, chapters in books about study, and lists of "dos and don'ts" for studying. They explain that you need a nice warm comfortable room, good light, no radio or TV, no wandering thoughts, plenty of paper and sup-plies, and time. And of course, the proper assignment. Many of you know that all these physical things can be in place, but after the first two or three tries of a new school year it just doesn't work. Potato chips are added, the radio is on low, the phone rings for just one call, or a TV special is on from eight to nine that night. In other words—planning the study time and place and being there aren't the same as doing the work.

DOING THE WORK

Plan the amount of time you are going to work or study. Don't let yourself get away with changing the time after you have made just one phone call or visit with a sister or brother. Figure out exactly what you want to accomplish with a specific goal for each subject. So many problems in mathematics, so many pages of history to outline, so many words to memorize in French. If you have one hour for each subject, and you start with mathematics, when the hour is up and you are only half finished, go on to the next subject. Don't use all three hours on mathematics! Either you didn't understand the assignment, or it is too hard and the whole class won't get it either, or you aren't going to make it in math. At least not tomorrow. Go on to the French for the next hour, and to the history for the third hour. If there is time left over after working on all three subjects, go back to the mathematics. *Organize* your time. Experience will help you with this, and your time will be used more effectively when you stick to allotted times. You have heard that people with the most to do get the most done—it's the same principle. If you have all day to clean your room, you can take all day to do it; if you have to clean it in one hour in order to go to the movies, you can do it in one hour. Don't let yourself spend all night or all day on one assignment.

Plan which assignments you will do in what order. Some students start with their favorite, in order to get going faster, and others begin with their least favorite, in order to get it over with so that they aren't too tired at the end with the worst subject left to do. After an hour at your desk, take a planned five- or ten-minute break. Get a snack or talk to some one or turn on the music and walk around and stretch.

Don't wait until a subject interests you before you plan to do the homework! Until you learn enough about it—it couldn't possibly interest you. You have to do your social studies or Latin or geometry assignments whether you like them or not. And good students *become* interested in subjects because of study.

Even though the subject doesn't interest you, the best study takes place when you know why you are studying, you care about what you are studying, and you are certain you can actually do the work. Try to understand the work for its own sake. Learn how *you* do in the subject; not how much you have to do in order to please a teacher or to get a particular grade.

Memorizing

No matter how modern the school you attend, or no matter what the latest fashion in learning is, you can't get very far without memorizing. There is vocabulary to memorize, scientific formulas, events, names of people, authors of books, characters in literature, dates for historical periods as well as specific dates of events to learn. You can't write a good examination without specifically memorizing information.

There are some helpful tips for memorizing. The most obvious is that the more you understand about what you are trying to memorize, the easier it is to remember. Learning nonsense *is* difficult! And many students try to memorize nonsense simply because they haven't taken the time to understand the concept in the first place.

Concentrate on what you are trying to memorize and use as many senses as possible to learn. Read the material aloud so that you can hear as well as see it. Don't try spending long hours at a time, beyond your efficiency for memorizing. Fifteen- to twenty-minute sessions with other homework in between the memorizing sessions are the most effective way to memorize for most students. Going over the memorization just before class is always a help—not to learn but to recall the poem or facts or vocabulary.

Testing

You will periodically be tested on the materials you covered during the school term. If you understand the subject you will be able to use your study time to review for these tests and examinations. If you have worked just enough to get by for your daily assignments, and you called that studying—then all your review time has to be spent cramming or learning the material for the first time! Cramming can work for one or two subjects, but it will never work for four of five strong subjects if you plan to do *well* in them.

A bright girl *can* attend classes, cram, and learn enough to pass a test in all her courses; but if academic work is something you want to develop and grow into a meaningful activity in your life, then studying *must* take a priority right *now*.

Learning

Actually, the word "learning" or "understanding" has more to do with you than the word "homework" (which sounds like it's for the teacher) or the word "studying" (which sounds like working for the sake of the work). If you think of studying as learning or understanding new things and people and concepts or discovery—it may help. You want all the help you can get for this skill of studying to learn on your own, as it has to be.

WHERE CAN YOU GO FOR MORE HELP IN LEARNING?

There is no substitute for the teacher of a course to help you to learn. Different subjects must be studied differently; to go to the mathematics or foreign language or history teacher is by far the most relevant help you can get. Don't be afraid to ask your teacher how to study to learn the particular subject. Most teachers will be pleased with your interest since usually teachers feel that the last interest students have is studying to learn. For this very reason many teachers don't teach you about studying. Don't wait until you are in a crisis to ask for help. Especially if it's a new subject and you aren't getting the understanding of it that you expected to have. Go to the teacher while it concerns *you*—not when your lack of understanding also concerns your teacher, your parents, and your counselor. By that time you are into reasons removed from you and learning.

Educational Decisions

The sooner you take your work seriously (learning), the sooner it will become very meaningful and worthwhile for you to be spending those three hours every night at it. You will be surprised at how interesting your work can be! Remember it is *you* who are learning and understanding. You are becoming a person who needs to know as much about your learning ability as you can in order to make those curriculum, educational, vocation, and career decisions that you will have to make.

Read to Learn

JOYCE SLAYTON MITCHELL

The image of women is a constant put-down in text-books, films, and school curriculum materials. For years, girls and young women must go to school and read about themselves as passive, dependent, and non-competitive people. It all begins in the elementary readers where Jane has to stand around and watch Dick run and have all the fun and where father always gets to drive the car.

In high school, textbooks teach women that they don't belong in many fields. One such is government and politics, according to Jennifer S. Macleod and Sandra T. Silverspoon. Their book, You Won't Do, *illustrates that "high school textbooks on government fail to discuss individual women, fail to quote women, fail to include women in their illustrations in reasonable numbers, fail to use women's case histories as examples, and mention the female half of the population only occasionally."*

The State Department of Education in Pennsylvania has reacted to the issue of unfair treatment of women in schoolbooks that degrade females and omit women's contributions to history, literature, and science. They have committed their department "to making the elimination of sexism in education a priority." A bibliography of feminist resources has been developed by the

Pennsylvania Department of Education. Included in this chapter is an adaptation of their first effort toward a positive image of women through a reading list suggested for grades 7 through 12.

The best readers read a lot! The more you read, the better you read; the better you read, the more you understand. Schoolwork and learning revolve around reading. It is the fundamental skill needed for you to become an educated person. If you plan to continue beyond high school, reading will be the crucial skill for you to possess—and *enjoy*.

Are you a good reader? Here are some things that will help you to know:

A good reader reads easily and fast.

She understands what she reads.

She remembers what she reads.

She reads groups of words—thought patterns—rather than word by word.

She reads at different speeds depending on the purpose of her reading (test, pleasure, contrasting ideas).

She has a good vocabulary and continually adds to it.

She reads critically and questions the source and purpose of the author. She doesn't believe "everything in print."

She reads all kinds and types of materials and books.

She loves to read.

Everyone can improve her reading. Most of us don't read as fast as we could because we have been taught to read slowly in order to get all the facts. Many students don't see any reason for reading any faster.

Nevertheless, you will get more and more reading assigned to you as you continue in school, you will get more interested in related books, and you will hear about books you wish you had time to read that aren't related to anything you are studying in school. The faster you can read, the faster you can finish your required reading and read something of your choice.

A good reader knows which materials to read fast and which will take more time. All reading shouldn't be at the same speed. If you are taking notes to write a term paper, or memorizing dates or formulas as you read—these things must be read more slowly. If you are reading the newspaper, a novel, or an essay, you can read much faster and learn to skim in order to get the main point. A good reader has learned to decide what speed is necessary for the job.

HOW TO IMPROVE YOUR READING

When you start reading, know what you are reading for: the main idea, particular facts, pleasure, to compare the same subject with another author, or for ideas to write something of your own. Learn to look at the reading material: its length, the names of the chapters, the headings used in the text, and the summary. This information will give you an idea of the style and organization of the author. Most articles can be understood by reading the opening sentence to find the problem the author is going to write about and the final paragraphs of his/her summary. Many things you select to read won't be what you had thought they were, so don't read them through after you know they are not what you needed. Learn to browse, to explore; try a book, and if you decide it isn't right then choose another one.

Push yourself to read faster, practice some rapid reading every day. Use a ruler and move it down a page at a regular rate and see how fast you can cover the page, trying not to move your head or say the words in your throat. All the physical motions with head and eyes and voice slow your reading rate. Look at as many words at a time as you can, and learn to give your full attention to what you are reading. Don't use your brain power to block out a radio program when you can use it to concentrate on your reading and your understanding of what you read. Really try to develop a fast and good reading style.

DEVELOPING YOUR VOCABULARY

Developing your vocabulary is a by-product of reading. You can't learn or understand any more than your understanding and knowledge of words will permit. The larger your vocabulary, the more you can understand what you read, and the more ideas you will have to express yourself in writing and speaking. Vocabulary is the most significant measure of a student's intelligence and ability to do well in school. If schools had to use only one test to predict success in school, they would use the test that measures vocabulary.

You may have heard about many methods to improve your vocabulary such as special courses, books, special schooling, and lists to memorize which increase your vocabulary in a week or a month. But the most logical and reliable way to build your vocabulary is by working with words as you read. This doesn't mean to interrupt your reading to look up every word you don't understand as you go along. If you can get the meaning of a word through context make a note of it and look it up when you have finished. Nothing could make reading more uninteresting than to stop with every few paragraphs to use a dictionary.

Nevertheless, figuring out the general meaning of words as you go along in your reading doesn't take the place of knowing exactly what the word means. Get the dictionary habit. Have a plan or a system for reading that includes writing words that you aren't sure about in a notebook—or looking up a particular number of words at the end of your reading. Keep your dictionary nearby so that you can get to it without looking all over the house, or going to someone else's room for it. Buy a dictionary written especially for high school or college students. Try to develop an interest in words, where words come from, when they are used; find the synonyms (very similar to) and the antonyms (opposite of) of the word in order to learn the shades of meanings. These synonyms and antonyms are found in a thesaurus (Greek word for "treasury"). A paperback edition of *Roget's New Pocket Thesaurus* should be on your desk right next to your dictionary. A thesaurus is easy to use. It is arranged in dictionary form and it's a must for your writing. For instance, when you are writing a book report or term paper, instead of using the word "marvelous" four times, look at your thesaurus and choose other related words or similar words for "marvelous": wonderful, fabulous, spectacular, remarkable, outstanding, prodigious, prime, splendid, superb. . . .

Reading develops vocabulary which develops ideas which enrich *your* life!

WHAT SHOULD YOU READ?

Most of you will have many teachers that assign all kinds of things to read so that you may never have to ask this question. Some of you, however, will have a chance to select your own reading materials from a list of assigned reading; and others will get no direction whatsoever for your reading.

Reading lists are only suggestions. A guide to your reading possibilities, rather than a rule about your decisions, is the intent of any reading list. Two reading lists are included in this chapter. The first is a feminist reading list adapted from the Pennsylvania Department of Education and the second is from the National Council of Teachers of English for those of you who are going on to college.

The Pennsylvania Department of Education compiled a feminist reading list as a first step toward eliminating sexism in their public schools. The books selected were evaluated on the basis of the American

Library Association standards and on the guidelines developed by the Pennsylvania Joint Task Force on Sexism in Education. Books selected for grades 7 through 12 are included here:

BIOGRAPHY

WILLIAM H. ARMSTRONG, *Barefoot in the Grass: The Story of Grandma Moses*

JOYCE BLACKBURN, *Martha Berry*

IRWIN BLOCK, *Neighbor to the World: The Story of Lillian Wald*

SUSAN BROWNMILLER, *Shirley Chisholm*

FLORENCE HORN BRYAN, *Susan B. Anthony*

HENRIETTA BUCKMASTER, *Women Who Shaped History*

OLIVE W. BURT, *First Woman Editor: Sarah J. Hale*

MARY STETSON CLARKE, *Bloomers and Ballots: Elizabeth Cady Stanton and Women's Rights*

FRANCES C. CONN, *Ida Tarbell, Muckraker*

LOUISE CRANE, *Africa: Profiles of Modern African Women*

DEBORAH CRAWFORD, *Four Women in a Violent Time*

ALLEN F. DAVIS, *American Heroine: The Life and Legend of Jane Addams*

BURKE DAVIS, *Amelia Earhart*

ETTA DE GERING, *Wilderness Wife: The Story of Rebecca Bryan Boone*

ESTHER M. DOUTY, *America's First Woman Chemist: Ellen Richards*

JEANETTE EASTON, *Narcissa Whitman: Pioneer of Oregon*

PHYLLIS HOLLANDER, *American Women in Sports*

MINA C. AND ARTHUR KLEIN, *Kathe Kollwitz: Life in Art*

ROBIN MCKOWN, *Marie Curie; The World of Mary Cassatt*

MARGARET MEAD, *Blackberry Winter: My Earlier Years*

ANNE MOODY, *Coming of Age in Mississippi*

CARMAN MOORE, *Somebody's Angel Child: The Story of Bessie Smith*

ELIZABETH P. MYERS, *Madam Secretary*

IRIS NOBLE, *Israel's Golda Meir, Pioneer to Prime Minister*

PAT ROSS, *Young and Female: Turning Points in the Lives of Eight American Women*

PHILIP STERLING, *Sea and Earth: The Life of Rachel Carson*

RICHARD STILLER, *Queen of Populists: The Story of Mary Elizabeth Lease*

ELFREDA VIPONT, *Towards a High Attic: The Early Life of George Eliot*

OCTAVIA VIVIAN, *Coretta: The Story of Mrs. Martin Luther King, Jr.*

WINIFRED WISE, *Fanny Kemble: Actress, Author, Abolitionist*

FICTION

ANNE ALEXANDER, *Little Foreign Devil*

PATRICIA BEATTY, *Hail Columbia*

CAROLE BOLTON, *Never Jam Today*

ALAN BURGESS, *The Inn of the Sixth Happiness*

ELEANOR CAMERON, *A Room Made of Windows*

HILA COLMAN, *The Girl from Puerto Rico*

CAROLINE CRANE, *Don't Look at Me That Way*

ANN FINLAYSON, *Rebecca's War*

CONSTANCE C. GREENE, *A Girl Called Al; Leo the Lioness*

ISABELLE HOLLAND, *Cecily*

JULIUS HORWITZ, *The Diary of A.N.: The Story of the House on West 104th St.*

JESSE JACKSON, *Tessie*

CARLI LAKLAN, *Migrant Girl*

EVELYN LAMPMAN, *Go Up the Road*

DORIS LESSING, *The Golden Notebook*

CARSON MCCULLERS, *The Member of the Wedding*

ELIZABETH GEORGE SPEARE, *The Witch of Blackbird Pond*

BETTY UNDERWOOD, *The Tamarack Tree*

ELIZABETH GRAY VINING, *The Taken Girl*

VIRGINIA WOOLF, *Mrs. Dalloway*

HISTORY

OLIVIA COOLIDGE, *Women's Right: The Suffrage Movement in America*

ELEANOR FLEXNER, *Century of Struggle*

GERDA LERNER, *The Woman in American History*

TREVOR LLOYD, *Suffragettes International*

EDYTHE LUTZKER, *Women Gain a Place in Medicine*

ANNE FIROR SCOTT, *The American Woman: Who Was She?*

JANET STEVENSON, *Women's Rights*

ELINORE PRUITT STEWART, *Letters of a Woman Homesteader*

LITERATURE AND THE ARTS

MAYA ANGELOU, *I Know Why the Caged Bird Sings*

ANNE LINDBERGH, *Bring Me a Unicorn*

BETH KLEIN SCHNEIDERMAN (ed.), *By and About Women: An Anthology of Short Fiction*

FRIEDA SINGER (ed.), *Daughters in High School—An Anthology of Their Work*

STEPHANIE SPINNER (ed.), *Feminine Plural: Stories by Women about Growing Up*

ROSEMARY SPRAGUE, *Imaginary Gardens: A Study of Five American Poets*

MEL WATKINS AND JAY DAVID (eds.), *To Be a Black Woman: Portraits in Fact and Fiction*

SOCIAL SCIENCE

KAREN DECROW, *The Young Woman's Guide to Liberation*

ELSIE M. GOULD, *American Woman Today: Free or Frustrated?*

LUCY KOMISAR, *The New Feminism*

MARGARET MEAD, *Sex and Temperament in Three Primitive Societies*

TONY MERRICK, *The American Woman: Her Image and Her Roles*

JOYCE SLAYTON MITCHELL, *I Can Be Anything: Careers and Colleges for Young Women*

The National Council of Teachers of English is a professional group of English teachers from all over America who are concerned about what students read. They have published a list that was prepared by asking English teachers of first-year college students what they think high school students should have read before they got to college. The list is arranged alphabetically —not according to the most important books.

Some books are deleted and new ones added to the list as students react to what they have read and as teachers change. The best list available for the college-bound student is the following *Suggested Precollege Reading:*

SHAKESPEARE—PLAYS

1. *Julius Caesar*
2. *Hamlet*
3. *King Lear*
4. *Macbeth*
5. *Romeo and Juliet*

POETS
British

1. W. H. Auden
2. William Blake
3. Robert Browning
4. Robert Burns
5. Lord Byron
6. Geoffrey Chaucer
7. Samuel T. Coleridge
8. Thomas Hardy
9. Robert Herrick
10. Gerard Manley Hopkins
11. A. E. Housman
12. John Keats
13. John Milton
14. William Shakespeare
15. Percy B. Shelley
16. Alfred Lord Tennyson
17. Dylan Thomas
18. William Wordsworth
19. William Butler Yeats

American

1. e. e. cummings
2. James Dickey
3. Emily Dickinson
4. T. S. Eliot
5. Robert Frost
6. Allen Ginsberg
7. Langston Hughes
8. Robert Lowell

9. Marianne Moore
10. Edgar Allan Poe
11. Ezra Pound
12. Edwin Arlington Robinson
13. Theodore Roethke
14. Carl Sandburg
15. Walt Whitman
16. Richard Wilbur
17. William Carlos Williams

PROSE

1-2. Suggested, above all others in this section, the Bible—at least a substantial portion of it—and Homer's *Odyssey*
3. Jane Austen, *Emma*; *Pride and Prejudice*
4. James Baldwin, *Go Tell It on the Mountain*
5. Samuel Beckett, *Waiting for Godot*
6. Charlotte Bronte, *Jane Eyre*
7. Emily Bronte, *Wuthering Heights*
8. Albert Camus, *The Stranger*
9. Lewis Carroll, *Alice in Wonderland*
10. Rachel Carson, *The Sea Around Us*
11. Willa Cather, *My Antonia*
12. Cervantes, *Don Quixote*
13. Eldridge Cleaver, *Soul on Ice*
14. Joseph Conrad, *Heart of Darkness*; *Lord Jim*
15. James Fenimore Cooper, *The Pathfinder*
16. Stephen Crane, *The Red Badge of Courage*
17. Daniel Defoe, *Robinson Crusoe*
18. Charles Dickens, *David Copperfield*; *Great Expectations*; *Oliver Twist*
19. Fyodor Dostoevski, *The Brothers Karamazov*
20. Ralph Ellison, *Invisible Man*
21. Ralph Waldo Emerson, *Essays*
22. William Faulkner, *The Bear*
23. Henry Fielding, *Joseph Andrews*
24. F. Scott Fitzgerald, *The Great Gatsby*
25. Benjamin Franklin, *Autobiography*
26. William Gerald Golding, *Lord of the Flies*
27. Graham Greene, *The Power and the Glory*
28. Thomas Hardy, *The Mayor of Casterbridge; The Return of the Native*

29. Nathaniel Hawthorne, *The Scarlet Letter*
30. Joseph Heller, *Catch-22*
31. Ernest Hemingway, *A Farewell to Arms*; *Short Stories*; *The Sun Also Rises*
32. Hermann Hesse, *Siddhartha*
33. Homer, *Iliad*
34. Victor Hugo, *Les Miserables*
35. Aldous Huxley, *The Brave New World*
36. Henry James, *The Turn of the Screw*
37. James Joyce, *A Portrait of the Artist as a Young Man*
38. John Knowles, *A Separate Peace*
39. Malcolm X, *The Autobiography of Malcolm X*
40. Herman Melville, *Billy Budd*
41. Arthur Miller, *Death of a Salesman*
42. Mythology. Bulfinch's or Hamilton's collection
43. Eugene O'Neill, *Long Day's Journey into Night*
44. George Orwell, *Animal Farm*; *1984*
45. Francis Parkman, *Oregon Trail*
46. Alan Paton, *Cry, the Beloved Country*
47. Plutarch, *Lives* (selections)
48. Edgar Allan Poe, *Tales*
49. Ole Edvart Rolvaag, *Giants in the Earth*
50. Edmond Rostand, *Cyrano de Bergerac*
51. Jerome D. Salinger, *Catcher in the Rye*
52. Bernard Shaw, *Androcles and the Lion*; *Pygmalion*; *Saint Joan*
53. Sophocles, *Antigone*; *Oedipus Rex*
54. John Steinbeck, *The Grapes of Wrath*
55. Jonathan Swift, *Gulliver's Travels*
56. Henry David Thoreau, *Walden*
57. John Ronald Renel Tolkien, *The Lord of the Rings*
58. Mark Twain, *Huckleberry Finn*; *Life on the Mississippi*
59. Virgil, *Aeneid* (especially books 2, 4, 6)
60. Thornton Wilder, *Our Town*
61. Tennessee Williams, *The Glass Menagerie*
62. Richard Wright, *Black Boy*

HOW DO YOU CHOOSE BOOKS
FROM THE LIST?

Nothing is worse than trying to select a book for a required reading report by just picking a book by its title and knowing nothing more about it! It's making a decision on the basis of almost nothing. Again, the National Council of Teachers of English has prepared a paperback book, *Books For You,* to help high school students with their reading selections. It is well worth 95 cents if you can't find it in your school library. It is an annotated guide to books for high school students. An annotated guide means that it gives one or two lines of description about the book. For instance, if you select Jane Austen's *Pride and Prejudice* from the Precollege List, *Books For You* describes it on page 15: "In this early nineteenth century comedy of manners, Mrs. Bennett's ambition was to find husbands, preferably wealthy, for her five daughters; but there were many crises before any of the girls reached the altar." Here is a description of Hermann Hesse's *Siddhartha*: "The search for communion and contentment within the framework of Indian mysticism is the subject of this moving, human statement first published in 1922." *Books For You* will help you to select books for required reading as well as for fun. If you can't find it at your local library, write to Washington Square Press, Simon and Schuster, 630 Fifth Avenue, New York, N.Y. 10020.

For those who aren't interested in reading and who are not going to college after high school, there is a wonderful book that will end your search for the thinnest book possible for your required English class book report; it is called *High Interest, Easy Reading.* The National Council of Teachers of English wrote this book for students who can read but just aren't interested. Even though these books are easy to read, they are written for high school students. If your library doesn't have a copy of it, send 95 cents to Scholastic Magazines, Inc., 50 West 44th St., New York, N.Y. 10036. Ask them to send you the 1972 edition of *High Interest, Easy Reading.*

Like most reading lists for students, this book is a sexist book (it lists separate books for boys in the categories of adventure, mystery, and sports while almost all the books for girls are listed under love and romance). But knowing this about book lists and about many school personnel's book recommendations, go ahead and look in any section (boys or girls) that interests you for a book to read.

WHAT CAN YOU LEARN ABOUT YOURSELF THROUGH READING?

There is no limit! Every subject that interests you—such as chapters in this book about religion, sexuality, or drugs—is just a beginning compared to all the written materials you can find and read in depth about each topic. You can learn how others your age and from other parts of the country or world think and act and how they behave in the same situation. You can learn about travel and people and animals and projects and how to build a house. And all the while you are reading you are learning about your reaction to things that sound like you, to things that don't sound like you, and your reaction to where you are in the range of topics you read about.

You can soon learn that it's not only you who has trouble explaining your feelings to others; it's not only you who is worried about what you will do in the summer, or when you get out of high school, or what to do about contraception. It's not only you who are concerned and consumed with all the things that you can't talk about, or when you do talk about them to your friends they don't know any more than you do about them.

Reading brings to you the whole world of other people's experiences and discoveries that you will want to be in on as you are in the midst of decisions about your own world of experiences and discoveries.

Tests Are One Measure

DOUGLAS D. DILLENBECK

Douglas D. Dillenbeck, editor of The College Handbook, *is executive director of publications for the College Entrance Examination Board. His work has always reflected his first concern: the student—you.*

A high school woman best understands the results of her test scores when she knows the difference between test scores for males and test scores for females. If your school uses a traditional occupational or interest inventory test such as the Strong Vocational Interest Blank, Kuder Occupational Interest Test, Ohio Vocational Interest Survey, or American College Testing Inventory, and they have separate forms for male and female—then your test results are sex stereotyped. The interests and occupations suggested to you are female stereotypes which assume that women are inclined to be passive and are best suited for tedious, routine, and repetitive work.

This sex-role bias in tests is unfair; it assumes that women have a natural preference for nursing, teaching, home economics, and social work. Test results reinforce what little girls have learned from their elementary readers: girls do not excel and should not compete in complex, high-prestige occupations outside the home. Added to this injustice is the vocational developmental work researched almost exclusively on boys and men, which causes vocational counseling as well as testing to be much less scientifically based for girls. Again, the assumption is that male *research and* male *tests and* male *behavior equal human behavior; females must adapt as best they can.*

Even such non-sexist tests for intelligence, ability, and achievement as the College Board scores can be used for sexist purposes. For instance, when a small, private, coeducational colleges wishes to keep a majority of male students or a particular ratio of men to women, they either lower the admission test standards for men, or raise the standards for women, or take a higher percentage of men than women from their qualified applicants. In one very well known competitive college in the East, 27 men applied with a College Board SAT score above 750; almost all (25) were accepted. In the same group of applicants were 58 women above 750 SAT; less than half (26) were accepted. In a similar college, 51 males were accepted with less than 500 SAT; only 11 females with those scores were accepted. This common practice is hard on everyone because the professors give the same amount of work and expect the same quality of performance from all students. Male and female students quickly polarize with the men harassing the women for "working too hard," and "keeping the grade point average too high" —as if the bright female students are trying to flunk out the men! With this attitude go the slights and humiliations toward women for being academic achievers.

As you learn more about tests in this chapter you will learn that test scores cannot be your only basis for a good decision. Mr. Dillenbeck writes that tests give you just one piece of information about yourself—not the whole picture. Still, that bit of information about you may not be used in the same way—by counselors or by recruiters for jobs, schools, and colleges—as it is for your brother.

When the teacher tells the class there will be a test tomorrow, everyone moans and groans and carries on as if it were the end of the world. Most people are only half serious when they act this way about a test —it doesn't really bother them that much because they usually do all right on tests. Some people really mean it, though. Tests worry them. They're afraid they won't do well, or they may even fail. Then the teacher may criticize, other students may laugh (or sympathize, which is even worse!), and their parents may be angry or disappointed. It's no fun to have other people finding out about your faults or weaknesses. If that's the main thing you think about when someone mentions tests, you probably worry about them too.

There's another way to think about tests that has more to do with *your* learning. No matter what reasons other people may have for giving you tests, you can use them, too, to get information about yourself. That's always a good thing. The more you can know about yourself, the better you can figure out what kind of person you are and can become. Tests can show you that you have abilities you may not realize. They can also show you weaknesses that you aren't aware of. Either way, you're better off when you have a good measure of these strengths and weaknesses than if you don't know about them.

When you find out you're especially good at something, you can begin to think about the best ways you use that ability. Most of the famous singers, athletes, dancers, and other kinds of performers that you know about discovered their special abilities when they were no older than you. Most scientists begin showing their special interests and abilities quite young, too. Some writers have their first books published only a few years after they finish high school. It's not too early for you to be thinking about what you want to do and be. Tests can help you do this.

SOME KINDS OF TESTS

Most of the tests you take in school are made up by your teachers and given only to their own students. A teacher may say that tomorrow your class will have a test on the chapter you just completed studying in your textbook. Or maybe it's the end of the report period, and s/he gives a test to help determine the mark you will get on your report card.

The other main kind of test is the printed kind that your school buys or rents from outside, called a "standardized test." These may be given to all the students in your school—or perhaps just to all the students in your grade—usually not more than once or twice a year.

Teacher-made Tests

The test that your teacher makes up usually consists of a few questions or problems taken right from the material your class has been studying. It may ask you to remember certain facts, like important dates or the names of people or things, or it may ask you to write what you think about some subject, or it may give you certain problems to solve. After the teacher has marked all the test papers, s/he usually returns them to the class so you can see how well you (and everyone else in the class) did on that test. This gives you two kinds of information about yourself. First, it shows how close you came to measuring up to the teacher's expectation. If your mark on the test is 80, it means you answered correctly about 80 percent of the questions that the teacher thought you should be able to answer. Or, if your teacher uses a different system of marks, you may get a mark of *B,* which usually is a way of saying that the teacher judged your test paper "good."

It's nice to know how well you are meeting each teacher's expectations, but you have to be careful about how you interpret that information. Do you know some teachers who seem to expect a lot from students and have the reputation of being "hard markers"? Their tests may be long and difficult, and very few of their students get high marks. Do you know some teachers who are "easy markers" and give out a lot of high marks? Most people have had both kinds of teachers by the time they reach high school. Because teachers give different kinds of tests—some easy, some hard—and mark them differently, too, you have to remember that your mark on a teacher's test is just *that* teacher's rating of your work—not anyone else's. A different teacher might have given you a test with easier questions, and you'd have gotten a higher mark. Which mark would be right?

The other kind of information you may get from a teacher-made test is how you compare with the other students in your class. If you know what marks the others got, you can see whether you were one of the highest, one of the lowest, or around the middle of the group. When you make this kind of comparison, it doesn't matter if your teacher is an easy marker or a hard marker, because you all took the same test and got marked by the same teacher.

You can't tell very much about yourself from just one teacher-made test, but after you have been in class for several months and taken quite a few tests, you should begin to get a picture. Are your test marks in this class *usually* around the average? Never mind if an occasional mark is much higher or much lower. Are your test marks in this subject usually higher or lower than your test marks in other subjects? Are your test marks in this subject this year generally higher or lower than those you got in the same subject last year? These are some of the ways you can look at your teacher-made test marks for useful information about *you*.

Standardized Tests

In some schools a student is given several standardized tests every year, beginning around the third or fourth grade. In other schools, this kind of test may not be used at all. Even if you have never taken one, you should read about them, because you will probably take some in the next year or so, and they may be very important to you.

A standardized test is one that has already been tried out on hundreds or thousands of other students to be sure that the questions are clear and to find out how hard or easy the test is. Most tests of this kind have a lot of questions—50 or 100 or even more—but the questions are short so you can answer them quite fast.

Very often the questions are "multiple-choice," which means that you just have to pick out the best answer from four or five possible answers that are given for question. Here is an example of a multiple-choice question: The opposite of *flexible* is (A) soft (B) rigid (C) unsteady (D) angry (E) fragile. The best answer is (B), *rigid*, because it comes closest to meaning just the opposite of the word *flexible*.

Standardized tests are often printed in booklets that can be used over and over again. You are given a separate sheet to mark your answers on—usually by filling in with your pencil a space with the same letter as the answer you chose. For example, you would answer the question given above by filling in the circle marked (B). If you haven't taken standardized tests before, you might be put off at first by these special ways of presenting the questions and recording your answers. You will get used to them, though, and then you'll be able to appreciate the convenience of being able to answer the questions by just making a pencil mark instead of having to write out a lot of words and numbers.

Usually your answer sheet will be sent somewhere

else to be "scored" by a machine that can count your right answers and wrong answers with practically perfect accuracy. It may be a few weeks after you take the test before your school gets back a report and passes it along to you. By then it may be hard to remember what the test was like, but you should try, because that will help you to understand what your score means. (What you get on a teacher-made test is usually called a mark or a grade, but on a standardized test it's a score.)

WHAT SCORES TELL YOU

Standardized test scores come in many forms. They begin with some person or machine counting the number of questions you answered correctly and sometimes the number you answered incorrectly or didn't answer at all. These counts give your paper a number called a "raw score," which doesn't mean anything all by itself, so usually you don't even get told what your raw score is. For example, you might take a test with 96 questions, and you get a raw score of 62. If that's all you knew about how you did on the test, would you think you had done well or poorly? But now suppose you are told that only 5 ninth-grades in every 100 get a raw score as high as 62 on that test, and all the others—95 percent of all ninth-graders—get lower raw scores than that. Now what would you think about how well you had done?

The number 62 tells you nothing, but 95 percent tells you a lot, and that is one way your score may be reported to you. It is called a *percentile,* and it tells you what percentage of some group of students you did better than. When your score is reported to you as a percentile, you always need to know what group it refers to, so you can say that you did better than, say, 95 percent of some particular group. It might be all the ninth-graders in the country, it might be all the students in your school who are taking ninth-grade mathematics, or it might be just the students in your school who are applying for a special class in college-level biology. In fact, your score might be compared with the scores of several different groups, and you would get a different percentile for each group.

Instead of a percentile rank, your score might be given to you in form of a *grade equivalent score*. This kind of score is used quite a lot with elementary school tests in various subjects and skills, like reading and arithmetic. They are used in high school, too, sometimes, but this is harder to understand because students study different subjects in high school. You may have taken tests called "achievement tests" in elementary school, and you—or more likely your parents— were told that your mathematic score was "at the tenth-grade level." That sounds as if it means that you could do tenth-grade mathematics when you were only in the sixth grade, but you know that it couldn't mean that. What it really means is that you answered the questions on that test—mostly the kinds of mathematics problems that you had studied in the sixth grade or earlier—as well as the average tenth-grade student would answer them. That's not a very useful kind of information, but it may be the only kind of report you get from some tests. You can still compare your own scores with those of your classmates to get a general idea as to whether you came out high among them— or low—or around the middle. And you can use a simple rule to turn a grade-equivalent score into a similar comparison with students of your grade all over the country. If your grade-equivalent score is about the same as the grade-level you are at, your score on the test is about average. Any higher grade-equivalent means above-average performance on the test, and the higher the grade-equivalent score, the farther above average it is.

One other way that scores on standardized tests are often reported is called a *scaled score*. This just means that the raw scores on a test have been converted to numbers in a certain range or scale—usually so the scores on different tests can all be put on the same scale and compared with each other. Scaled scores, like raw scores, don't tell you anything all by themselves, so whenever your test results are reported as scaled scores, you will probably be given percentiles, too, or else tables in which you can look up various percentiles for your own scaled scores.

NORM GROUPS

This is a term you may hear or see when you are finding out how you did on a standardized test. It's important for you to understand it. The norm group is the whole population you are compared with when your score is turned into a percentile or a grade-equivalent score. Usually on a test of school ability or achievement, the norm group will be the girls and boys in your grade all over the country. Sometimes it will be just the girls (and a boy's scores will be compared with just the other boys' scores). Sometimes, especially if you are in a big school or a big school system, the norm group will be just the other students in your grade in your own school or city. Sometimes, on a test of interests—which may not be called a test, but instead, a questionnaire, or inventory or preference record—your scores will be compared with those of adult women in different occupations.

Which norm group is used for comparison can make a big difference in how high or low your scores stand, so you must always know about the norm group in order to interpret your scores.

HOW OTHERS USE TESTS

Teachers and counselors use standardized tests not only to measure each student's abilities and school progress but also to learn about the whole group of students in the school. They might find out, for example, that their seventh grade is falling behind the national population of seventh-graders in arithmetic skills, and they might decide to try to remedy this in the eighth-grade mathematics classes.

Usually, though, such tests are given to help them learn more about individual students. A test can help them to understand someone's special learning problem, for example, by showing some weakness in a particular learning skill. A diagnostic test in arithmetic might show that you were fast and accurate in adding, subtracting, multiplying, and all other kinds of computations with the whole numbers but that you made mistakes almost every time you had to divide with fractions. Knowing this, the teacher could then concentrate on teaching you division with fractions and not waste time on other things at which you were already good.

Teachers and counselors may also use tests to identify your strong points and perhaps to plan special activities or classes to help you develop your best abilities even better. Teachers usually know your strengths and weaknesses pretty well after you have been in their classes for a while, but tests help them get to know you faster. They also help the teacher to learn to know you better if you're a very quiet student with special problems or abilities that would not be noticed in regular classwork and assignments.

TESTS FOR JOBS AND COLLEGE

When you apply for a job or for admission to college, you may be asked to take a certain test, or maybe a whole series of tests. The employer or college will use these, along with other information about you, in deciding how to answer your application. The employer wants to find out whether or not you have the ability to do satisfactory work in the job that you are attempting to fill. Or if there are several applicants, the employer may be trying to decide which one is best suited for the job. The college admissions officer, too, is trying to be sure that the applicant has the ability to succeed in the college. Or if there are many more applicants than the college has room for, the admissions officer may be trying to decide which ones are best qualified.

There are two other ways that many colleges use tests, and these may be very important to you some day. One way is for placement, or deciding what courses you would benefit from. A college might place you in a remedial class in English composition if your records, including certain test scores, seemed to show that you needed to learn to write better. Or it might let you go right into a sophomore English course in your freshman year because you showed that you had already mastered the skills and knowledge that are taught in its freshman English course. When a college lets you skip over some beginning course and go right into a more advanced one, that is called *advanced placement*.

The other important use many colleges make of tests is to give credit for college work that you learned outside college. For example, if you are a good writer and qualify for advanced placement in English, the college may also give you college credit for the freshman course it lets you skip. Some very able students who have learned college-level work in several subjects while they were still in high school find that they can enter college as sophomores and save a whole year's time and expense.

USING TESTS TO HELP YOURSELF

Even though you usually take tests only because someone else wants the information about you that they give—a teacher, counselor, a college, an employer—it makes sense for you to use the information, too, for your own benefit. There will even be a few times while you're in high school when it will make sense for you to take certain tests just for your own use, even when they are not required by anyone else.

The main reason for this is that some tests are the best means available to get certain kinds of information that you need in making decisions and plans about your future. If you are thinking of going to a certain college and want to know how your scholastic abilities compare with those of the students who go to that college, the best way to find out is to take the same test of scholastic abilities that the students at the college have already taken and compare your scores with theirs. If you are trying to choose between two colleges and can make this comparison with each one, you may see that you would stand much higher in ability among the students at one of the colleges than at the other. That information may enable you to imagine some important differences in what it would be like for you at each college. This may be reason enough for you to choose one over the other.

As you go through high school, you may have the experiences of being high, low, and average in ability compared with the other students in various classes. You may find that one of these situations brings out the best in you. Perhaps you respond well to the challenge of having to work hard to keep up with the other students, who find the work easier than you. Or maybe you get discouraged in such classes but do your best work when you can have the satisfaction of being one of the best in your class. Or maybe it doesn't make much difference to you what the other students are like. How you react to such situations may give you an important clue to how you will fare at college—and perhaps to something you should look into when you choose a college. Tests can help you do this.

One more way you may make use of tests for your own benefit is to build up a record of your academic achievement—especially if your high school record, for some reason, is inadequate. Perhaps you lived abroad for some years and learned a foreign language that doesn't even show on your school record because you never studied it in high school. A test in the language might be the means for you to get it on your record that you have this skill, which you may want to be able to prove some day. Or perhaps you go to a school that is practically unknown to colleges because it's small or new or because very few of its graduates have ever gone to college. In any of these cases, a college admissions officer might not know how to evaluate your school record because she wouldn't know how well you have been taught or what standards your marks represented. But if she also saw your scores on the admissions tests that she was familiar with, she would then have some evidence that she could understand about your ability and preparation for college.

SOME TESTS TO KNOW ABOUT

Here is a list of tests you will hear about while you're in high school. As a rule, it will be up to you to decide whether or not to take these tests and when to take them, so it would be good if you knew something about them.

1. *Preliminary Scholastic Aptitude Test/National Merit Scholarship Qualifying Test (PSAT/NMSQT).* This test is given every October in most high schools, mainly for juniors, although anyone can take it who wants to. It's like the College Board Scholastic Aptitude Test (SAT) that hundreds of colleges require, so it gives you a chance to see what the SAT is like and how well you can do on it. It takes two hours, and you get two scores—a verbal score to show how good you are with words and language, and a mathematical score to show how well you handle numbers and quantities. You can compare your PSAT/NMSQT scores with the SAT scores of applicants and freshmen at the colleges that require the SAT. They're published in a directory, *The College Handbook,* which all high schools have for their students to use. If you take the PSAT/NMSQT in your junior year, you will also be

considered for the scholarship programs administered by the National Merit Scholarship Corporation.

2. *Scholastic Aptitude Test (SAT)*. This is one of the admissions tests of the College Entrance Examination Board, required by about a thousand colleges of applicants for admission. It is given at test centers all over the United States and in other countries around the world on five Saturday mornings every year. Your own school may be a test center, or you may have to travel to the nearest test center at some other school or a college. The test takes three hours, and you get a verbal score and a mathematical score, like the PSAT/ NMSQT scores. Your school gets them, too, so they can help you with plans for college. And your scores are also sent to the college or colleges that you ask to have them sent to. You can have them sent to colleges later if you don't know where you want them sent at the time you register for the test. You should take the SAT in the spring or summer of your junior year in order to get the most benefit from it. That way you get your scores early enough to use them when you're deciding what college or colleges to apply to. Also, if they happen to be lower than you think they should be, you still have time to take the SAT again and try for higher scores. If you don't take it in your junior year, though, you can take it in the fall or winter of your senior year, and that's early enough for most colleges.

3. *College Board Achievement Tests*. These are the other admissions tests of the College Entrance Examination Board, required by several hundred colleges. They are one-hour tests in fourteen high school subjects, and as a rule you would take only two or three of them, depending on what was required by the college or colleges you were applying to. Some colleges give you a choice, and you pick the ones in your best subjects. The Achievement Tests are also given at College Board test centers on certain Saturdays. Usually you wouldn't take any Achievement Tests before

the spring of your junior year or winter of your senior year, but you might want to take one as early as the spring of your sophomore year if you were taking a subject that year—say, biology—that you would not take any more of in high school and you thought you might have use for a good test score in this subject.

4. *American College Testing Assessment Program (ACT)*. This is an admission test of the American College Testing Program required by many colleges for applicants of admission. It is given at test centers throughout the United States and in several foreign countries on five Saturdays during the year. It takes about four hours, and you get scores in English, mathematics, social studies, and natural sciences.

5. *Advanced Placement Examinations*. These examinations in college freshman courses are offered by the College Entrance Examination Board and given by high schools to students who have taken special college-level courses in high school or learned the equivalent knowledge in some other way. Colleges may use your grades in these examinations to let you skip the corresponding freshman courses in college and even, in some cases, to give you credit toward your college degree. In some colleges, a student who has gotten satisfactory grades on three or four of these examinations may enter as a sophomore and complete her undergraduate program in only three years instead of the usual four years. The examinations take a half-day each and are given during one school week each May.

6. *College-level Examinations*. This is a program of examinations in college subjects, administered during the third week of each month at test centers throughout the United States and at military bases overseas. Although originally developed to serve adults who needed a way to show colleges or employers that they had learned the equivalent of certain college courses in their work experience, by independent study, or by some other means, College-level Examinations are being used by colleges more and more as a basis for granting col-

lege credit to incoming freshmen. If you have special knowledge of some subject that is commonly taught in colleges for credit, you might want to look into the possibility of taking the appropriate College-level Examination and getting college credit for it.

TAKING TESTS WITH THE RIGHT ATTITUDE

Like most tools and instruments, tests can be used well or poorly, and their use can be helpful or damaging. The main thing for you to remember is that each test gives you just one piece of information about yourself—never the whole picture—so you should just add that information to everything else you know about yourself. If other information you have seems to contradict the test score—for example, if you get a low score on a test of something you've always been quite good at—the chances are that the test score is wrong. Don't believe the test score if you have better evidence of some other kind.

Even though you may get the impression that the purpose of tests is to keep you out of courses, programs, colleges and careers, keeping you out is NOT their purpose!

If you think about tests with a healthy skepticism and as only one of many possible measurements, you will see that there's less reason than you may have realized to be nervous or fearful when you take a test. Tests aren't mystical. They can't come up with an answer about you or your ability that isn't there. The more aware you are of your academic abilities and interests, the less surprise a test score will be to you. Being very disappointed or elated when you find out your test scores should be about like the way you react to a grade in a term paper or book report. They are all part of your evaluation.

Think of tests as information along with your marks, teacher comments, and your own evaluation and interest in a subject. Information that can help you make sound educational and career decisions. Information that will permit you to choose appropriate plans for your future.

Curriculum Choices

JOYCE SLAYTON MITCHELL

Schools spread sexism. Some ways are very easy to see: there are more high school males than females playing sports; there are more males than females in the student government and in school leadership roles; there aren't many women described in your history books; a story about a man means a story about all humankind's struggle with truth or nature, but a story about a woman means a story about a woman and her struggles with truth or nature; and the number of pictures showing women in your government textbooks will range from 3 to 9 percent of all the book's pictures.

Not so plain to see, and therefore more dangerous, is the attitude of some educators that you won't really use your education unless you are a failure—a failure, that is, in your primary role of wife/mother. In the meantime, you will fill in your time with school and jobs rather than make a serious commitment to your educational and career decisions. School reinforces the idea that a woman's educational and career choices are stopgap decisions. Many women think, "I'll go to college until I get married," "I'll take a job (or go to graduate school) until I get married," "I'll take a job until I have a baby," "I'll take a job until I get remarried," "I'll take a job until my husband retires." All these choices are stopgaps—something to fill in the time until something better (more romantic and initiated by someone else) happens.

In spite of the attitude toward you that you don't really need your education and therefore don't need to make a long-range commitment, you can learn to think of yourself as a person who does need her education. Being a husband and father doesn't interfere with long-range decisions for males; being a wife and mother doesn't have to make your decisions short-term either.

The purpose of high school is for you to find out exactly what you can do in different subjects and how well you can do it. The discovery for you includes all levels of technical education, all levels of mathematics, all levels of physical sciences as well as the foreign languages, social sciences, and clerical courses that you already know about.

You do need your education. You need it for success. Success in whatever turns out to be your choices.

Curriculum is what educators think high school is all about. Curriculum means the courses or subjects offered in the high school program. It is the reason to have high school, the core or heart of the school. It is the academic or educational part of your growth and development that the school is organized for. True, many high school students would find a complete life without curriculum because of their time and interest in sports, clubs, newspaper, music, cafeteria, and each other! All these activities do keep students busy, and it is often easy to forget that curriculum or course work is supposed to be the central theme of everyday high school life.

If you live in the suburban or urban areas of America, it is possible to have over five hundred different courses to choose from as you plan your high school program. As with all choices, the greater the number of choices, the greater the difficulty to choose.

There are many ways to think about your high school

program. The most common way to select your course of study is to answer the often asked question, "What do you want to do when you get out of high school? A teacher, an engineer, a nurse, a lawyer, a social scientist?" With a career answer, the counselor then says, "You will need this course and that course," and your curriculum choice is all solved. Or you will answer the other question most often asked, "What college do you want to go to?" You will look at the college catalogue, a general description of requirements will be listed, and once again, most decisions of subjects to study in high school will be made.

"Where are you going after high school?" or "what are you going to be?" become the counselor's questions to you rather than what program you will select in high school. Choosing high school courses by what you want to be while still in the eighth grade can lead to many problems. The biggest problem is that you can't possibly know what you want to do when you don't know your options! And how can you possibly know your options when there are all kinds of things to be you haven't even heard of? And how can you know what you want to be when you have seen only a few different jobs compared to the many available, and you have talked to even fewer people in those jobs! What happens if you change your mind? Most of you will change your mind—not once but over and over again. As you grow and learn more about your academic abilities and your interests, you will change your idea of all the things that are possible for you. That change is not taking place in a vacuum; the world of work and the tradition for what girls and women can do in the world of work are changing rapidly.

Let's not take the most common way to go about choosing high school subjects. Let's forget what you are going to do or be or where you are going to go five years from now. Let's concentrate on what you want to learn right now that will lead to your knowing a range of possibilities for your life. Let's plan a high school curriculum so that the only doors that will be shut to you will be shut by your abilities and interests and personality.

HOW TO SELECT YOUR COURSES

What is the most logical way for you to select your high school courses? Like all things in education, the future depends upon past record. The most significant way to choose your subjects for next year is by your school record and what you can learn of your test results. If you are in a school that groups eighth-graders or freshman English classes according to ability and you are in a top group, you will want to take the strongest academic program the school offers *regardless of what you want to be or where you want to go after high school*. If you are in the lowest group of eighth-graders you will want to take a program that permits taking the very minimum requirements for continuing education after high school. If you are in the middle group of eighth-graders or of a high school class you will try what areas you can do well in and pursue those in depth. As soon as you find out that mathematics (Algebra and Geometry) or foreign languages aren't for you, take the two minimum years and go on to get more subjects in your stronger areas of study.

Even if you have your mind set on being an engineer, and you have a *D* in Algebra I and a *D* in Geometry, remember that requirements to be an engineer don't mean *taking* three or four years of mathematics, it means taking and having the ability to do *well* in three or four years of mathematics. Often career choices sound good because of what the picture of an engineer, or doctor, or social worker looks like in your mind, with little regard for your ability. Don't get stuck with the picture! Be flexible with your ideas of courses so that you are free to leave an idea after it proves not to be a good one, and you are free to go after an idea that is new because you have learned a new skill and interest. Chances are, with a *D* in two years of mathematics, or a *D* in French I followed by a *D* in Spanish I, it isn't the teacher, and it isn't that you didn't put in enough time. Those subjects just aren't for you.

If you are in a school where a teacher or counselor will discuss your test results with you, you will want to consider to some extent the results of your reading, language, readiness tests for algebra, foreign languages, and achievement tests in certain areas. Most educators will agree that no decisions should be made on test scores *alone,* but they may show you that you have more ability than you have shown in your work and should give algebra a try. Usually, of course, your test scores coincide with your marks. When you are selecting eleventh- and twelfth-grade courses and have test scores that are much higher than your marks, chances are that you have already established your pattern of not studying because you aren't that crazy about studying. If you aren't terribly interested in schoolwork, then high test scores aren't very meaningful for predicting success in school. In other words, if by the time you are sixteen years old you still use "not studying" as an excuse for poor marks, you should realize that you'll probably never enjoy studying as your major activity.

In addition to your past marks, test scores, and the help a counselor may give you in choosing your subjects, your teachers can be very useful in helping you decide what you can handle. Talk to your teachers when you can't decide whether to continue in a particular subject. The more ideas you can get about your work, the more information you will have for your final decision.

As you select your curriculum, always keep in mind the purpose of high school. Don't forget why you are there, and how curriculum fits into your life; it's you who are becoming a person, and part of the person you are becoming is an educated and thinking person. You are not in high school because that's what teenagers do, but because you want to find out exactly

what *you* can do with your life and how well you can
do it.

STRONGEST PROGRAM

What should a high school program be like for a
bright student who works hard and needs the strongest
program available? A strong freshman program in a
forward school (one where Algebra I and a foreign
language begins in the eighth grade) will include English, Algebra II or Geometry, Biology, one or two
foreign languages depending on the eighth-grade program, and a social science if a strong course is offered
to freshmen or if it's required or if it's needed as a
fifth academic subject.

English	Biology (or a strong
Algebra II (or Geometry)	science)
Foreign Language II	Foreign Language I
	Social Science

Your choices in this program are which foreign languages to study and whether to take Earth Science or
Ecology if Biology isn't offered to freshmen.

A continuation of the strongest curriculum program
would be:

Second year:

English II	Social Studies (or one
Math III	of options below)
Foreign Language	Chemistry (or Biology
	or Foreign Language)

Third year:

English III	Foreign Language
Math IV	American History
Physics (or Chemistry or Foreign Language)	

Fourth year:

English IV	Foreign Language
Math V (college level)	(college level)

| Foreign Language (or one of the options below) | Advanced Placement Science (or Physics or Social Science) |

In the above illustration the student will continue with a foreign language or a social or physical science depending on how she does with previous courses, her interests in her courses, and the particular courses her high school offers. *These are not decisions to be made in the eighth grade,* but rather ones to be made after completing some work in these fields. They are also not decisions to be made on the basis of sex; girls should *know* that they can take and do well in mathematics as well as foreign languages and physical science as well as social science. All bright students (girls and boys) should take four years of mathematics or four years of one foreign language or in-depth in all subjects when they are doing well simply to find out how well they can do in academic work.

If you have to choose between Mathematics IV or V or Physics, a good rule is to take the math. All college mathematics and physical science are based on mathematics, so the more mathematical background you have from high school, the better understanding of science you can develop when you are in college. Most engineering colleges and physical science professors who teach college freshmen advise students to take mathematics if they must make a choice between physics and mathematics. However, most top academic students can take both.

FOREIGN LANGUAGES

There are so many options in foreign languages that often students can't decide which language to take or how many years of each to elect. Most educators agree that it is better to learn one foreign language in depth rather than take two years of two different languages, as was advised years ago. For the strong academic student, however, keep in mind that the Ph.D. candidate must take a reading examination in two foreign languages, so that many feel a reading knowledge of two foreign languages is better than a reading and speaking knowledge of one language. For most students, the reading part is often overstressed in school. Students want to learn to talk and sing and communicate in a foreign language and not have to read the longest book list, as most foreign language is taught.

A basic question for students is whether to take a classical or modern language, which usually is a choice between Latin I and French or Spanish I. Most language teachers would agree that if you are going to take a classical and a modern language, you should begin with the classical language. If you have had no previous foreign language, you could begin with Latin in your freshman year and continue with it the next year. If you have started French or Spanish in the eighth grade, you can continue the modern language in your freshman year and begin Latin the same year. The rule that you begin only one foreign language at a time does have exceptions, and if you are especially good in languages and everything in your schedule works out best by beginning two foreign languages at once, then go ahead and begin them!

The decision you have to make about which modern foreign language to take is a difficult one because it is really a matter of preference rather than one of principle or best education. Usually you can choose between French, Spanish, sometimes German, less often Russian. If you live in Maine or Vermont and are close to French Canada, or in Texas or California and close to Spanish-speaking Mexico, or NYC with many Spanish-speaking people, it would make most sense to learn the language of your geographical heritage. If you begin one of the modern languages in elementary school, usually you would be best off to continue that particular language before starting another.

If you think that one foreign language is much easier than another, or you have trouble with French but have heard that Spanish is easier—BEWARE! The only differences may be in pronunciation. Learning any new language—learning the structure, verbs, and idioms of a different language—needs the same kind of regular study habits, the same understanding, and the same language ability. Who teaches the language will make more of a difference in how hard or easy the French or Spanish is than the language itself. Here again, if your high school is in rural America and offers only two years of Latin and French, or if you are an exceptional language student and all the options of your school are not enough, remember you can get home-study courses from accredited universities in Chinese, Russian, Hebrew, or college French.

SCIENCE

In talking about science programs, often the question arises about when to take the College Board Achievement tests in science. For instance, most students study biology in their second year of high school, and if they are considering using biology as a college board score, by all means they should take their achievement test in biology at the end of the year when they complete the course, even if it is in their freshman year. It wouldn't be very valuable to the student or to the college to have a test score in achievement one or even two years after a course was completed.

MINIMUM COLLEGE PREP PROGRAM

Let's say you have the *worst* marks in eighth grade for anyone who wants to go on to school after high school; you are at the bottom of your class. Your test scores aren't good, but you think if you work as hard as you have this year you could probably take the minimum academic program and pass. You want to continue your education at least to a two-year program, and you want to find out what you can do and what you can't do and where your interests lie.

The minimum requirements for continuing education in a college preparatory program will be four years of English, two years of higher mathematics (Algebra and Geometry), one lab science (Biology usually counts), and three years of Social Science.

There are also one- and two-year community colleges, trade, technical, and business programs beyond high school that will accept applicants with commercial subjects, and a general high school program without Algebra.

For most two-year programs in a college, the following high school program is necessary:

First year:
English I   General Science
Social Science   elective

Second year:
English II   Social Science
Algebra I   elective

Third year:
English III   American History
Geometry   elective

Fourth year:
English IV   Social Science
Biology   elective

Foreign language is not mentioned because many good schools in the country do not require a foreign language. If you have a hard time in English, and language is a problem for you, then foreign language is out of the question. If your language ability is fair and you are encouraged to take a modern foreign language, then take Algebra I in the ninth grade, Geometry in the tenth, and a foreign language in the eleventh and twelfth grades. DO NOT TAKE ALGEBRA AND A FOREIGN LANGUAGE TOGETHER in your first year of high school if you are not a good student. If you improve by the time you are in the eleventh grade, and it does happen, then take the foreign language at that time. Learning a total new language structure and higher mathematics requires more abstract thinking than your junior high school subjects required. If you don't do too well with the concrete, don't plan to take the abstract!

Most high school students will not take either of the programs illustrated because most of you will follow a program somewhere between these two extremes. Many subjects have not been mentioned that almost all students take: physical education, music and art, typing and business subjects, driver education, and trade and technical courses, depending on the type of school you go to and the part of the country you live in. These subjects all count. They interest you, you need a level of skill in physical education, typing, and fine arts, and the levels offered you vary from school to school.

Even though you write out a four-year program in the eighth grade, feel flexible and free to change it as you go along. Don't get stuck with an eighth-grade decision about how many years of science or foreign language you "need." What you really need is to know how well you can do these things. When you find this out you can make your selection of subjects according to what you know about what you can do.

NUMBER AND LEVEL OF SUBJECTS

How many subjects should you take? The idea that you make better marks if you take fewer subjects, usually doesn't work out that way. Most honor roll students take the most number of subjects. If you are an *A* or *B* student in the eighth grade, you should probably take five subjects; if you are less than that, maybe four academic subjects one year and five the next, depending on what the subjects are. Some of you will make that decision on the basis of other things you are doing—how many hours you spend in sports, in music lessons, in clubs, how many hours you work outside school, and how much time you spend sharing home responsibilities with your family.

Don't think that because your minimum requirements are satisfied by your senior year, you should take three academic subjects and elect art or driving or music in place of a fourth or fifth academic subject. The freshman year of college will be a full schedule, and it is important to prepare for this year by taking a strong senior year in high school. If you have been an *A* or *B* student, hang in there with strong academic subjects. On the other hand, if you have worked very hard and come through with a *C* average, the senior year is a good time to get the nonacademic courses that you haven't been able to think about before now.

If you have a chance to be in an advanced program and you wonder if you would be better off with a *B* in Advanced Chemistry or an *A* in the regular course, you will be interested in knowing that most colleges prefer a *B* in the advanced course. In addition to the grade, the teachers in the advanced courses are often more enthusiastic about planning their course, and the course usually has extras in equipment and priority in the school budget. Advanced courses often have many "hidden" benefits that make them very much worth the extra effort on your part. If, however, advanced work makes you feel dumb and second-rate, it isn't worth your time. You won't be asked to join the class unless you have top academic qualifications. But it doesn't make sense for you to take a course that makes you feel like borderline intelligence, when really you are only borderline for an advanced group of students.

IT'S YOUR CHOICE!

Often your parents and teachers will disagree with what subjects you should take. The best thing to do in that case is to try to hear everyone's point of view. As you listen to different ones giving their advice on curriculum, be sure to recognize their interest in the subject. For instance, a French teacher will tell you French is the thing, while a Spanish teacher will tell you Spanish is better.

As much as students would like to feel that the school, the counselor, or their parents are responsible for their high school curriculum choices, the responsibility is really yours. You can't tell someone ten years from now that you didn't become what you wanted to because "someone" didn't tell you the best things for you. It is always your final decision to drop a course, to elect a new one, to try to change teachers, to take on extra work, to sluff off. All the advice from all the people who are quick to give you opinions will not be a substitute for your decision.

Select carefully, it's *your* high school record we are talking about. Finding out what *you* can do educationally is what curriculum choices are all about.

Discovery through Sports

NATALIE M. SHEPARD

Title IX makes it against the law for schools that receive federal funds to discriminate against females in educational activities and programs. Even in athletics. Nowhere is the regulation more controversial than in this area. Many educators and coaches have organized to try to make an amendment to say that sports don't apply in this law, that it's ridiculous to put as much money, time, and energy into girls' sports as into boys' sports.

If we know that students learn best about competition, cooperation, leadership, and friendship from playing team sports, then we want girls and women in on these positive values too. It is only justice that they have the equality in learning and experience through sports that are provided by public school funds. Scientific facts researched by and for men to keep girls out of Little Leagues and young women from using federal funds in education because they "prove" that girls aren't strong enough, healthy enough, big enough, protected enough, or fast enough will no longer be accepted.

Professor Jan Felshin, of the Pennsylvania NOW sports committee tells us the consequences of separation in sports: "As long as women in sports are kept in exclusive categories, we will not know the effects of

*the most sophisticated training, the finest coaching, the
highest aspiration, or the serious dedication. Contemporary sport is not equal, and therefore its continued
separation insures that male superiority will be upheld
and women will be denied access to equal opportunities
for self-esteem and actualizations. Where prejudicial
and discriminatory attitudes already prevail, separate
cannot be equal, and, in fact, confirms the sexist assumptions."*

*Dr. Natalie Shepard integrated physical education at
Denison University and in her chapter assumes the
possibility of sophisticated training, fine coaching, and
high aspirations when she writes about self-discovery
through sports. Professor emeritus at Denison, Dr.
Shepard is an extraordinary teacher. Her first lesson to
her students has to do with discovery and integration
—of mind and body with soul.*

Members of the human race have engaged in competitive sports since the dawn of time, and almost without exception the sports world has been the sole pos-
session of the male. But a variety of interacting forces
has brought changes so significant that woman has
challenged this exclusiveness. Male domination of competitive sports is out.

No single factor can be cited as being solely responsible for all the interest in competitive sports for women. But television with its marvelous coverage of sports
events, and particularly of national and international
sportswomen in a variety of sports, has provided examples to the youth of America. Especially too, in the
coverage of the Olympic Games, where women like
three-time gold medal winner Wyomia Tyus have com-
peted with spectacular brilliance and acceptability, the
examples have been persuasive and attractive. Five years
after her remarkable Olympic record, Tyus has emerged
as the top woman in pro track. The message of
this whole new world of sports for women has been
spoken about in millions of homes.

Our culture has been clear about what is acceptable and what is nonacceptable behavior for girls in the world of sports. To watch and applaud the male athlete in his world of competition is prescribed and encouraged. But to acquire skills in the same sports world so that a woman might successfully compete, challenge, and even win in a contest with her male counterpart has been unacceptable. With the changes and challenges of the 1970s, however, old sexual stereotypes are questioned and prejudicial barriers are being torn away.

WHAT IS SPORT?

Sport is many things to many people. For some it is the same as games and means any activity from children's run and tag to the recreational pursuits of adults. For others it means only the "major" sports of high school, college, and the pro circuits. But what about water skiing, sky diving, jogging, and backpacking? Are these sports too? What about skiing and snowshoeing, swimming, fishing, boating, tennis, and golf? Does the activity need to demand strenuous physical exertion? Must it be competitive; or can it include fishing, camping, and watching TV? Are you a sportsperson only if you participate, or can you be a watcher and belong too?

In the first place, sport includes physical exertion and, in the main, sports mean activity. Whether we watch or play, strenuous physical effort is involved in every game. situation.

In the second place, sport is a clearly defined task set apart from the ordinary. A code is developed to which all agree. This code establishes the rules and one enters the "set-apartness" voluntarily. If you don't agree to the game, you don't play. For example: Here is the equipment, one ball, one pair of skis, one racket, one club; here is the playing area, one field, one tennis court, one mountain, or one pool; here are the rules and regulations, the prescription of what one may or may not do and how one shall behave. Here too is the goal or purpose, what shall be attempted and under what circumstances and restrictions. The essential question, the challenge, the impelling fascination: how well can the person do what is prescribed? Within these limitations how well can one perform?

In the third place, the sports world contrasts sharply with the ordinary, everyday world. In sport there is the freedom of choice. Much of life means jobs that are necessary and required, but the sports choices are voluntary and therefore much more fun. Furthermore, life is so complex that we always have to divide our attention. But the sports world presents a single job on which all of one's being can be focused. It *feels good* to focus one's whole self in this fashion, to get free from being pulled in a dozen different directions. For the short period of the game experience there is no fragmentation, no divided attention. One can experience being a whole person. Human beings *need* to exercise their bodies, need to use their human capacities for movement and energy expenditure, need to experience the exhilaration of complete wholeness, of being all of one piece!

WHY PLAY SPORTS?

I suspect that all the reasons that can be brought forward can be placed under the single heading of fun. *Look* magazine once ran an article under the title "Ordeal of Fun" and described with beautiful inclusion the many facets of the world of recreation and sports: the beauty, the pain, the challenge, the adventure, the risk taking, the rustic pleasure of a rural setting, the whole lovely gamut of things people do because it is *fun*. Why will you play sports? Why the delight in these activities that run so close to madness in their compelling urge to perform? Self-knowledge, Competitiveness, Stress and Risk taking, Fascination of the Unknown, Health and Fitness, and Belonging are some of the reasons.

Self-knowledge

Surely part of the reason for living is to know one-self. How you achieve this self-knowing has been the subject of endless speculation, meditation, and thoughtful analysis by the prophets of all time. All of life's experiences contribute to it, and so, too, the world of sports has much to offer. Some would say that the game situation presents *unique* opportunities, a special laboratory, because the whole self is involved. Your complete attention and enthusiasm are focused on a single task and thus the sport experience is integrating.

If you wish to know yourself, or another, put yourself in a position of stress. There is anxiety, fear, challenge, a chancy situation where failure is possible and very real, where success is possible and very real, and where the result depends entirely on a situation where *your* efforts, your skill, your competence make the differences. Try bicycling down a steep gravel road where acceleration takes you even faster, and a skid means a fall and physical injury. But a skillful passage means exhilaration, no skid or fall, the thrill of your own achievement and new confidence in yourself. For the "other," or for yourself, what is revealed in the experience of your relationships in this ride? Is there bullying, ridicule, impatience, unkindness if there is injury? Is there openness, caring, kindness? Is there pleasure in the success of the other person, patience with failure, generosity in the difference exposed by the achievement? Does not even a game of cards make some of the same revelation? Greed, intent to win at all costs, cheating when the chance arises; or generosity, fairness, helpfulness for the one who is just learning? The list of meanings in these game and sport situations is as endless as the gamut of human emotions, and as revealing.

Stress and Risk Taking

Sports provide varying opportunities for us to know ourselves in moments of stress—certain sports more than others, although almost any sport provides some of this element. The element of risk taking and of stress seeking is illustrated in any sport where physical exertion is required. You train, you condition yourself to peak physical health so that you can give yourself with abandon, making the difficult look easy, with perfection as the only goal and also the only safety. Failure hazards life and limb and the thrill is in the risk taking. You sky dive, spelunk, drive racing cars, rock climb, stunt fly, ski sail, skin and scuba dive, high jump and pole vault, swim and race to exhaustion. You do these things because it *feels good* to expend yourself completely, to use your human abilities to the utmost.

Among other sports, the Outward Bound Programs of three-week sessions are designed precisely for the experience of self-knowing under stress. Gradually skills are developed and the body conditioned to the peak of your physical capabilities. In addition, living together during the sessions, you seek new understandings of reliance on others and new experiences of confidence in yourself. Putting it all together, the final purpose of all the preparation is found when tests of risk taking and adventure are designed to reveal the self-knowledge of your own outer limits. The whole purpose is to test the limits of your endurance—not another's but your own. When you are there, the person you wrestle with is yourself, your own fear, your own courage, your own strength. Every personal resource is utilized until you stand naked before your own self-knowing.

In moments of stress, when all excuses or pretenses are stripped away, stress and risk taking in the sports world reveal you to yourself. You perform on the uneven parallels risking everything in the speed and disciplined abandon of your flying dismount, or you lead higher than ever before on your hurdle for the exacting forward one-and-a-half sommersault with full twist from the diving board. You catch the ball, or you fumble it; you have the staying power when the climb is steep, or you haven't. It is your skill, your training, your courage that makes the difference. This is the reason the stress and risk taking are thrilling; the pride in your accomplishment is against real, not phoney odds.

Our society does not value nonproductive activities. When the person has climbed the mountain and reached the peak, when the vault or the dive is made with the breathtaking beauty of the human form in motion and the action is completed—what is there to show for it? People are sometimes killed in their sports adventures, and society mourns their passing as a pitiful waste of human potential. WHY do people risk their lives in these seemingly senseless tasks? The answer lies in the self-knowingness. The explanation is in the *process* of the whole wonderful experience rather than in the "nothing to show for it," nonproduct aspect at the completion of the action. To DO it is enough. To be involved, to focus, and the completeness of expending oneself is an altogether experience. An integrated action. One that leads to the person's self-knowing and the recognition of her personhood.

Fascination of the Unknown

All sports contain the unknown. It is part of risk taking, part of the chanciness of the outcome of a contest, part of the stress and the yet to be revealed ability or nonability to sustain effort in the circumstance. The fascination of the unknown is the self-propelling ingredient in any game situation. Who will win, who will lose, who has what it takes, who is not ready for the contest?

Other aspects of the unknown are superbly inherent in an environment that is out of the ordinary; that is, in the world of water and aquatics, or the world of air and sky diving, or the world of the wilderness in contrast to our cities and towns. Some sports are at home in these environments.

Consider the world of aquatics and the exploration of the unknown in its environmental qualities. To learn to swim and dive, to understand the nature of this medium, to water ski and boat, to sail and white-water canoe—there is excitement and thrill here. What fascination as its wonders are revealed! What freedom for adventure and for challenge lies in the achievement of basic skills in this water medium!

In the same way consider the way of the wilderness. It is not for all, but for those who train themselves in the skills needed to enjoy it, it is a lifetime of pleasure and satisfaction. Adventure and challenge in ever widening horizons beckons the explorer. The skills to enjoy it are too numerous to list but must include something of camping and survival activities, hiking and backpacking, mountaineering, nature study and ecology. So many facets of beauty are filled with the fascination of the unknown. Here is meaning and here reasons for being in the world of sports that uses the wilderness for its playing fields.

Health and Fitness

Until we are deprived of good health, who ever heard of doing things that we know are good for us just because we should? Health and physical fitness can and must be achieved, not as a goal, but as a by-product. As you play the sports you want to play, fitness and well-being come naturally through your activities. You keep in condition, you watch your weight and your nutrition, you exercise and condition your body *so that you can participate well*. Your purpose is to play the game, to perform with excellence, to be able to go the limit and not tire—to play, and play, and play again.

It's a little bit like happiness, or laughter, this being healthy and fit. If one seeks it for its own sake, it eludes one. Happiness and laughter cannot be forced. They come as a by-product of living with joy and abandon and giving of oneself, of living and caring and good friendships. Fitness and good health come in this way. The by-product of exciting, challenging, thoroughly productive good sports participation is glowing good health and fitness.

Belonging

Along with self-knowledge, the sports world offers the precious qualities of friendship and the chance to earn the right to belong. In no other situation is this human need more readily fulfilled. One enters the sports world by choice, a voluntary act, and in it joins with others in a world completely their own. This world is divorced from the ordinary, set apart with its own rules and prescriptions so that under no other circumstances are the requirements to belong more clearly defined. Do this task and do it well. If you achieve you are "in," you belong. Sport is color-blind and money-blind; performance alone is the coin of this realm. You cannot buy your way in. You belong because you can run faster, throw farther, dodge quicker. You can give laughter and make us all happier; you can encourage when we need that extra push. You lead and we follow because you can help us to win. Our battle may be against another team, against a machine or a mountain, or against ourselves. In spelunking you give us courage against the fear of the dark and the exploration of the unknown. In whitewater canoeing you give us strength when we need one more paddle push against exhaustion and a turn over. In skiing you go first and show us that it can be done. In basketball, when there are just two minutes left you have the courage and strength to stage a rally that gets us by with one point with no minutes to spare.

And when the exhilaration and the excitement of the game is over, we leave the sports world for the everyday world. We go back to our cultural divisions and our differences; but whenever we meet or remember, we "belong" together for that one thing we did, that one period we played together. We talk about it ceaselessly, we recall point by point, incident and moment by moment, the fun we had, the failure when we didn't quite make it, the joy of achievement when we did. Belonging is one of the most fundamental of human needs, and the sports world offers each person the opportunity to join. You bring yourself and offer what you have.

MORE READING ABOUT SPORTS

E. GERBER. *The American Woman in Sport.* Reading, Mass.: Addison-Wesley, 1974.

L. KLAFS. *The Female Athlete*. St. Louis: C. V. Mosby, 1973. A good understanding of conditioning, comp*e*tion and the current cultural attitudes toward the female athlete.

W. GERBER. *Sport and the Body*. Philadelphia: Lea & Febiger, 1972. A symposium by the leading authors of our day on sports and the body meanings inherent in sports participation, a philosophical approach.

D. HARRIS, ED. *Women and Sport: A National Research Conference*. University Park: The Pennsylvania State University Press, 1973. A remarkable resource for the student interested in the many aspects of the subject, women and sport. Excellent bibliography. Look here for what to read and where to find it. Contains writings from well known leaders and authors in the physical education and sports world.

The Sportswoman Magazine, P.O. Box 2611, Culver City, CA 90230.

WomenSports Magazine, P.O. Box 4964, Des Moines, Iowa 50306.

Awareness through the Arts
MONICA SCHLAG

Monica Schlag (pseudonym) is a violist who sometimes paints. At Northern Illinois University she helps non-musicians who may become teachers find their way in music so that they can help children find their way.

There is so much to be learned if you look within yourself and watch yourself in relation to others. It is essential to understand yourself, know yourself. Know why you do the things you do. Why certain things please you, why other things annoy you. Why you love, why you hate. Why you are envious, why you want to be like someone else.

One fertile place for you to begin this search, this looking, is in the realm of the arts that has aroused your interest so fully. Perhaps you love to sing or read poetry, play string quartets or manipulate tapes, listen to operas or play the guitar, work with electronic synthesizers or design cities, play with clay or assemblages, dance or look at paintings, or whatever it is. One real advantage in beginning here is that you won't have to force yourself to look. You will not have that determined kind of concentration which works against itself. Instead, there will be a kind of natural attentiveness and awareness which comes from doing something in which you are totally absorbed.

Interest in the arts—music, painting, poetry, drama and dance often draws us together—free-spirited young people with daring, imagination and creativeness.

Have you noticed that people who paint, sing, compose, or dance often look and listen in a peculiar way? They listen or look "comparatively." That is, they compare one performer with another, an early performance with a later performance, an artist's earlier work with his or her later work. They look with a comparative eye or listen with a comparative ear. Much music and art criticism is founded upon this kind of comparison, and entire books are devoted to it.

If we listen and look with a comparative mind, there is the chance we are missing much. Isn't it limiting if I say to myself, "Today I play viola like me but if I work really hard someday I may sound like Lillian Fuchs?" When we compare, are we hearing or seeing things as they actually are? Does it clarify or does it cloud our ability to hear or see? Since we must be very active and alive to catch the essence of an artistic work, is it possible when there is comparison?

It may be that such a "judgment and comparison" syndrome is a factor in one's dislike of, or annoyance with, any contemporary idiom. Imagine how disturbing it would be to listen to today's music of Pauline Oliveras with Ruth Crawford Seeger ears or to read the poetry of Emily Dickinson expecting Adrienne Rich or to view a Helen Frankenthaler painting with Mary Cassatt eyes.

If you have ever been involved in a dramatic production you will sympathize with the young actress who expressed her concern with the hours of rehearsal she was often involved in and the energy expelled in "going over and over" her lines.

Have you noticed when you're learning something—a skill, a piece of music, or a part in a play—that you seem compelled to repeat sections of it over and over again? Have you thought about the threat to creativity in too much repetition? Is it possible that undesirable mental and physical attitudes develop when you do something over many times? If you are not watchful and it becomes thoughtless reiteration you may well get locked into the very things you are trying to correct.

Then, of course, it takes twice as long to learn. Instead of so much repetition, if you can get a clear grasp of the material to be learned and approach it without anxiety and with self-confidence, surely there will be less distortion and fuller realization of the material as a whole. Sometimes, just visualizing and feeling how your body moves and your voice sounds away from the stage is more valuable than practicing the play over many times.

Of course, what we all work toward is the time when everything will fall into place with a natural flow and balance—your awareness, talents and efforts all working together.

I suppose one reason there is so much difficulty in all this is because of our indoctrination through years of schooling.

> We've learned to learn by repetition and drill. We've learned to learn by repetition and drill. People are always repeating things. People are always repeating things. They ask you to do something and then they ask you to do the same thing again. They ask you to do something and then they ask you to do the same thing again. Of course, by then you've learned there's no need to listen the first time because they will repeat it anyway. Of course, by then you've learned there's no need to listen the first time because they will repeat it anyway.

For some of you who follow your artistic interests, the freedom, excitement, and spontaneity found in the beginning are often lost because of the emphasis on so-called perfection and discipline. There seems to be a provocative contradiction in all artistic pursuits. If you are studying an instrument, for example, or learning to dance or paint, you have probably put yourself in the hands of a "specialist" and so the ideas of perfection and methods of discipline are hers and not yours. In fact, you may even feel that "perfection" and "ideals" have no real meaning in themselves and that you would rather be "perfectly yourself." So, as you see, the contradiction lies in the often oppressive and restrictive methods used in trying to bring someone else's ideal of beauty to fruition.

It's a joy to do something wonderfully well and that joy comes when perfection is the goal.

Have you ever known "an active participant in the arts"? Someone who listens and looks. You can possess a sensitivity and an awareness rare even in many practicing artists, dancers, poets, or musicians. You can listen to music the same way you listen to your friends or to a bird's song. And you can look at paintings and sculpture much as you watch the sun set or a butterfly on a leaf.

Each of us can begin to question how we listen, how we look. I have often wondered if we listened more sensitively when we were very young. There must have been a time when we listened to music much as we listened as a child to the locust's raspy song on a warm summer evening, or the haunting sound of the late afternoon wind blowing through the high grass on a Kansas farm, or the tinkling lobster buoys bobbing in the distant night waters in Maine—that is, *listening with every part of our being*. That must be what "active participant" means. Listening in which judgment and comparison played no part.

Although we may not be exactly sure what is communicated through them, sculpture and painting are also forms of communication. In the same sense, music too, may communicate—with the performer bringing an auditory communique from the composer.

Music, like any art form, has much to say to one who "listens." Just as when we speak our voice tells us something—sometimes quite different from our words. Notice the subtle way we use our voices, to soothe, to lull, to bore, to apologize, to impress, to implore. What music says to you may be something other than the intention of the composer or performer. Sometimes an artist, musician, or poet may even be saying with her work that she does not want to communicate. The next time you participate in an artistic experience you may want to see what you can learn about yourself from the "communion."

For some of you, your richest moments in life are nonverbal, often quite silent moments. Sometimes shared with another, sometimes alone. As with others of visual or auditory inclination, translating these moments into a verbal idiom may be difficult, while for the poet or playwright words are her paintbrush or bow. Many of you will come closest to revealing who you are as a human being through music or art. This revelation is not always realized, but when it is one hopes someone saw or heard and understood.

Is it surprising to you that creativity regarded to be really significant is always mentioned in relation to a painter, a musician, a poet, or a dancer? Surely a gardener, a teacher, a cook, a lawyer, or a mother can live creatively? And, of course, being in the "arts" doesn't assure that you will be creative.

As you look at this art you love, watch yourself with other people. The things you say. The things you do. How you feel. Instead of complimenting and condemning, try *just to look* and see what you can learn. It's all there within you.

Sometimes things become clearer when we ask ourselves questions, realizing, of course, the value will be in exploring the issues and not so much in the answers we find. Let's agree to bring only our own ideas or theories. Let's follow our own "score."

Other students have talked together about these questions. Here are a few they asked:

"Why do I paint?"
"Is it possible to do something because I love to do it and not for recognition and praise?"

"I wonder why I'm reluctant to have anyone see my poetry?"

"Can I listen to a compliment in the same way I listen to criticism? Fully and completely and then releasing the experience forever?"

"Why do I want to be famous?"

These are not yes or no questions, are they? They are rather fundamental questions and going into any one of them will be an arduous pursuit. But eminently and excitingly rewarding!

And my questions to you: Have you seen that your interest and involvement in the arts is not separate from your involvement in life? Have you discovered that the personal revelations born from artistic pursuits parallel those created in communion with other human beings and all living things? Will you give up dependence on authority and specialists and gain the freedom to look sensitively and questioningly at your own actions, relationships, and all that goes on around you with fresh, young eyes?

I know that many of you have experienced that kind of awareness and have felt tremendous joy in learning about yourself. It's learning that encompasses all of life, isn't it, not a fragment here or there? It means being a musician or a listener and *something more,* a dancer or a playgoer and *something more,* a composer or a sculptor and *something more,* an art lover or an artist and *something more.*

As you know, it requires an extraordinary awareness and sensitivity and it means responding to life not through arts, religion, science, literature, or athletics alone. Not just an intellectual, emotional, or physical response but a *total response* with your heart and whole being. In such a response you will find much beauty and great joy.

Educational Choices

Out of High School

Learning by Correspondence

JOYCE SLAYTON MITCHELL

Correspondence (Home Study) is available to you from kindergarten through college. Here are ideas about who uses Home Study, what kinds of courses are offered, how and where to get started. You may decide to learn by correspondence and take an advanced placement in mathematics, or an art course not offered in your high school, or to make up a failed Latin I course. You may decide to take a course in auto mechanics or selling real estate to get ready for a summer job.

The traditional way to education is through the local school system. We seldom think of other ways of education. There are other ways, and Home Study is one of them. Home Study education can be a nontraditional way for *you* to be where you want to be in your life. It can be your way to enrich and to further your education, or make up work, or get the necessary credentials you need for a job or your way to get your high school diploma without going to school.

WHO USES HOME STUDY?

You may be a very bright student who wants to add to the courses your school offers, or you may have failed a course and don't want to repeat it under exactly the same conditions as you failed it, or you may want a program in tax accounting or TV repair in order to get a part-time job. You may have taken a leave of absence to have a baby that has ended in a permanent leave of education. You may be a Spanish-speaking woman who needs a special English course designed just for you, or you may want to work half a day and study the other half in a setting other than the public school.

Home Study can be for the student who wants to study Chinese or Russian, or who wants a fourth year of Latin which her school doesn't offer. It is for students who want to go abroad with their parents rather than to boarding school. It is for high school students all over the country who want to learn more fine arts than their high schools offer or take advanced placement in mathematics or a course in ecology or even a course in plumbing.

Some of you live too far away from a school where you can continue your education, some of you have left school in order to bring home a paycheck rather than a report card, and some of you have been turned off by school and that was the end of it.

Now things look different. Your paycheck may be as low as your grades were, you may be unable to advance in your job without a high school diploma, you may find that having a baby at homes gives you enough free time to study but not enough time to attend classes. You can't afford to go to summer school to make up for a failure in mathematics, or you just can't see going through another year in regular English when you could be taking an advanced placement English course. Where can you turn? You know that your local school simply doesn't work for you. Fortunately for the 5 million students who need it and use it, Home Study is where you can turn.

WHY TAKE HOME STUDY?

It's so easy a solution that it often doesn't sound like its enough of an answer! It's cheap, it's easy, it works —and yet almost no one in the public schools thinks to recommend it. Correspondence courses started in America in 1890, and they have been used successfully by the armed forces for years.

Even though you may have lost out on other opportunities and been told it's too late, even though you don't have the latest fashions to wear to school, many of you can reach your goal through correspondence education. It can take the place of any other system or educational plan or add to your present educational course on a one-to-one basis, programmed for you and by you.

Home Study can be called programmed learning or independent study. The options in terms of courses, institutions, and costs include about three hundred institutions and one thousand courses.

The advantages of Home Study include your choice of times and places to study. You can do the lessons at your own speed; you can do them at home, at the local library, or wherever and whenever is best for you. The lessons you send back to the school will be corrected, graded, and returned to you with comments. Many of you will receive more help and personal attention than you ever received from the normal school system.

WHAT ARE THE DISADVANTAGES?

Educators often stress that the trouble with Home Study is that you must be a self-starter, you must have a definite goal, you must be a good worker, you must have self-discipline—and, they say, "most students don't." Perhaps most students aren't any of these things, but these very characteristics are the ones that many girls excel in. These are the characteristics that girls prove all the time as they work as hard as they do to get their work in on time, remember their assignments, do the required work, and end up with the best attendance, homework record, marks, and rank in class. Home Study learning is not for someone else to set up and organize for you. Home Study learning is for those of you who have decided you want and need another way to your education and career if the traditional way of learning doesn't work for you.

What are the specific educational opportunities to be found in Home Study? Home Study or correspondence courses offer everything from an elementary school diploma to language courses for a Ph.D. candidate! This includes junior high school courses, high school diploma programs, vocational and professional training, college courses for high school students and adults, courses for the physically handicapped, and courses for Spanish-speaking students.

WHERE CAN YOU FIND THE RIGHT COURSES?

How can you go about finding what is available and how to get started? Your first step is to select a school for the course or program that you want. Although you see advertisements for many Home Study and Correspondence Schools, you won't learn from such advertising which schools are educationally sound and which are not.

Many high school personnel say that correspondence schools are a fly-by-night operation out to get your money. To throw them all out because you can't tell the good from the bad is usually an excuse because the high school person isn't well enough informed about correspondence education. Reputable correspondence schools are accredited by two agencies that are approved by the U.S. Office of Education for this purpose: The National University Extension Association and the National Home Study Council. They make available to you—upon request—lists of schools, colleges and universities and their courses and programs approved by the U.S. Office of Education, just as your own school is approved.

The National University Extension Association publishes a *Guide to Independent Study*. Every college and university listed in the association's guide must be a member of their own regionally accredited higher education association, just as your own state university is regionally accredited. Even though the members listed are all names of colleges and universities, the courses they offer for high school students are especially designed for your age and reading ability. The National Home Study Council publishes a list of schools, courses, and programs for private Home Study schools.

High School students will find the following types of courses and programs offered by the National University Extension Association:

High School Diploma Program. A complete program for the student who wants to earn her high school diploma.

High School Equivalency Program. For the student who wants to prepare for the high school equivalency examination.

High School Subjects. For the student who wants general, business, secretarial, vocational, or college preparation subjects.

Vocational Training. For the high school student who wants a course in auto mechanics, drafting, woodworking, or electricity.

Certificate Programs. Designed for fulfilling specific vocational or professional goals in a special field of interest such as business administration, data processing, real estate, dental assistant, or training as teacher aide.

College Courses for high school students. College courses may be taken as preparation for college-level examination and/or credit for college work before starting college.

Specific courses which are included in the above programs range from remedial reading, writing, and English, to foreign languages taught with the use of tapes for study in French, German, Greek, Hebrew, Italian, Latin, Norwegian, Portuguese, Russian, Spanish, and Swedish for high school students taught on the college level. Mathematics courses offered on the high school level range from remedial mathematics courses to advanced placement mathematics, engineering mathematics, trigonometry, college algebra for high school credit, and theory of numbers.

In addition there are courses in study skills, anthropology, art, the Bible, government, history, journalism, music, religion, science, and vocational training which includes arc welding, auto mechanics, electronics, radio and TV repair.

Specific universities offering courses and programs for high school students are: The University of Wisconsin, Brigham Young University, The University of Utah, University of Texas, University of Tennessee, Pennsylvania State University, Oregon State University, University of Oklahoma, University of Nebraska, University of Missouri, University of Minnesota, Louisiana State University, University of Kentucky, University of Kansas, Indiana University, University of Idaho, University of Florida, University of Colorado, University of California, and the University of Arkansas. This list of twenty universities gives you an idea of the range of universities in America that offer correspondence education to high school students. There are sixty-two universities listed in the *Guide to Independent Study*. The ones cited are distinguished because they accept and encourage all overseas enrollments as well as high school-level students.

In order to obtain the *Guide to Independent Study,* send 75 cents to National University Extension Association, Suite 360, One DuPont Circle, Washington, DC 20036.

National Home Study Council

The National Home Study Council's list of private Home Study schools includes a wide variety of vocational and professional training courses and programs.

The private Home Study schools also offer high school courses and programs similar to the university programs. In addition their list offers a course for Spanish-speaking students written in Spanish, a course for teaching Braille to the blind, and a course for parents of deaf children.

Vocational courses for any age or educational level include: air traffic control, bus driving, camp management, fingerprinting, guitar playing, hotel operations, income tax preparation, millinery, mutual fund sales, stock brokerage, travel agent, yacht designing, and zookeeping.

The free list of private Home Study schools and programs is available from National Home Study Council, 1601 Eighteenth Street, N.W., Washington, DC 20009.

If Home Study education seems right for you, send to both of the above agencies for their guides and lists of schools and programs. Make a note of all the schools who offer the program or course that you want. Write to the particular school or college for their latest official requirements, fees, and admission information. If the course you want is offered both at a private school and a college, select the college because the credits are usually more readily recognized by other colleges, schools, or employers. Accreditation, and transfer of credits, are not the only reasons for taking a course, so remember that a private Home Study school may serve your purpose of independent study and learning as well.

AMERICANS ABROAD

If your family is going abroad for an extended time, a crucial question for you is, what will you do about school? There are many parts of the world without American schools or English-speaking schools. Places where schools start at a different time of year than the American time schedule or times when your family will not be staying a full school term. For these reasons, Home Study can be the answer for the American family abroad. Regardless of age, grade, time of year, number of children, correspondence education is available for the particular needs of any American family.

There are two American Home Study school programs on the elementary level of education. One is the Calvert School, Tuscany Road, Baltimore, MD 21210, approved and accredited by the state of Maryland; and the other is the Home Study Institute, Takoma Park, Washington, DC 20012, accredited by the National Home Study Council. Both schools offer a kindergarten through eighth grade program. Other English-speaking elementary correspondence programs that may be geographically closer to the family when you are away include Australia, England, and New Zealand.

Secondary education or Grades 9 through 12 can be completed through any of the high school programs listed under the National University Extension Association earlier in the chapter.

COLLEGE CREDIT FOR HIGH SCHOOL STUDENTS

Home Study courses are a natural way to prepare for college credit by examination. In order to encourage individual development there are others ways to receive credit from an accredited college. The College-level Examination Program (CLEP) of the College

Entrance Examination Board is an agency who gives proficiency examinations for college credit. Over five hundred CLEP testing centers are located throughout the United States and administer tests during the third week of each month. The fee for taking one examination is $15; for two it is $25. They report the results of the tests to you and to any college, university, or other organization you designate. There are presently more than fourteen hundred American colleges and universities that accept college credit by examination, and additional colleges are constantly being added.

This means that *you* can live anywhere in the world, work full time (including mothers with young children), and at the same time be earning college credits. You can take correspondence courses on the college level and prepare yourself for examinations and receive college credit completely on your own!

Remember, you don't have to qualify in any way. This program is especially for people who need a non-traditional way to receive college credit. It is for the bright, but not necessarily formally educated people. You don't have to be a high school graduate, you don't have to have the money or interest in a residential college, and you don't have to be free of family and economic responsibilities. The important point will not be how you got your education, but that you can demonstrate by examination that you have attained college-level understanding in a general or subject examination. For a free copy of further information about the CLEP program, write for *CLEP May Be for You,* CLEP, Box 1824, Princeton, NJ 08540.

COLLEGE DEGREE BY HOME STUDY

College-level courses are offered through the National University Extension Association. Every college or university varies in the number of courses or credit hours they will accept by correspondence toward your college degree. You can not fulfill the degree requirements of an American college entirely through correspondence. Every American university requires a student to spend some time on campus (called the "residential requirement") to earn a degree.

The University of London offers the only English-speaking recognized degree program with no residential requirement to fulfill for a degree. In other words, an American student living in the United States or anywhere in the world may work toward and earn her college degree without going to the university at any time. The University of London has been offering degrees by correspondence for over a hundred years. For further information, write National Extension College, Shaftesbury Road, Cambridge, CB2 2BP, England.

Summer Time Is Discovery Time

JOYCE SLAYTON MITCHELL

Here are summer ideas for camping, hiking, or biking; study or the arts; volunteer or paid work. Whatever your choice for this summer, it's a good time to try related or seemingly completely unrelated things to your school year. And it's especially a good time to discover that "it works" or "it doesn't work" for you. Use your summer experiences for one more input into your decision making for Other Choices.

What are you going to do this summer? How can you spend your summer to learn more about what you are like? School vacation can be much more to you than a time off from school! It can be an independent time for learning, an independent time for trying things out that you have learned about your interests and abilities and future plans during the school year. It can be a time for a practical experience that gives you a change from your academic experiences.

Your summer choice may seem completely unrelated to learning in school if you choose to make money rather than grades your goal; or to volunteer in an unrelated area of interest from anything you have been interested in before, like volunteering in a political office when your school time is directed toward a health career.

But nothing you do is unrelated to you. Everything you do—even the opposite interests from school interests—in work and play adds to your understanding of what you can do, how well you can do it, who you like to be with, and how well you like what you are doing.

Whatever choice you make for this summer—travel, camp, hosteling, wilderness trip, community service, study or selling—keep yourself open for changes in your interests and attitudes. It's a good time not to get stuck with, but to test, an idea about what you want to do with your life. It's a good time to try. Try working with younger children, raising money, surviving in the wilderness, working alone, working with scientists or bankers or volunteers, learning music with teen-age musicians, dancing with students from all over the country. And it's especially a good time to say "I like it" or "I don't like it" or "There are some things I like about it" or "There are some things I don't like about it." And to use these reactions for one more input into your decision making.

The best choice or job in the world for your cousin or friend may be the worst choice for you! It's *your* choice and experience—not what someone else says it will be like for you. Trust your summer experiences and your reactions to them as you learn how they relate to your understanding of you.

To help you think of ideas for your summer choices use this list to begin planning your summer. Each category includes specific examples and addresses where you can write for more information. Most information is free; send for it if you are giving any consideration to that particular summer activity. Follow up other leads and suggestions and read the newspaper and magazine classified ads until something sounds right for you. The more information you have, the better the basis for your decision.

CAMPING CHOICES

General Camps. A wide variety of sports and arts are offered in camps, usually for girls from 6 to 16 years of age. Ask about special groups for your age. A good place to start to look for a camp, other than your friends, is the Camp Directory in the *New York Times,* and in *Seventeen* and *Parents' Magazine.* You can also write to:

American Camping Association, 342 Madison Avenue, New York, NY 10017.

Association of Private Camps, 55 West 42nd Street, New York, NY 10036.

Special-interest Camps. Many older teen-agers go to a special-interest camp in art, music, aviation, dance; sports such as riding, tennis or sailing, or study in science, French, or conservation. Write *General Camping* for the addresses for special interests.

Work Camps. Work camps vary in their program from working all day to half a day's work with recreation, study, or religious activities for the balance of the day. Most of the programs are for both girls and boys and usually for older high school students aged 16 to 19. Many of the foreign work camps have a minimum age of 18 years. Write to the organization that has most to do with your church/synagogue, Scouts, or YWCA/YWHA for possible work camp choices. Check first with your local church/synagogue because the larger Protestant churches and Jewish groups have their own work camps. Write to:

American Friends Service, 160 North 15th Street, Philadelphia, PA 19102.

Girl Scouts of U.S.A., 830 Third Avenue, New York, NY 10022

National Council of Churches, Room 704, 475 Riverside Drive, New York, NY 10027

United Presbyterian Church in the U.S.A., Senior High Summer Program, 475 Riverside Drive, New York, NY 10027

United Church of Christ, Summer Service Projects, Pottstown, R.D. 2, PA 19464

Lutheran Youth Ministry Work Camps, 2900 Queen Lane, Philadelphia, PA 19129

Protestant Episcopal Elko Lake Camps, 38 Bleecker Street, New York, NY 10012

American Jewish Society for Service, Room 1302, 15 East 26th Street, New York, NY 10010

YWHA, 1395 Lexington Avenue, New York, NY 10028

Foreign Work Camps. Two clearinghouses for finding a foreign work camp situation are:

Vacation Work and Events Department, The National Union of Students, 3 Endsleight Street, London W.C. 1, England

Israeli Students Tourist Agency (work camps in kibbutzim), 2 Pinsker Street, Tel Aviv, Israel

HIKING AND BIKING CHOICES

Some of the nation's hiking clubs have special teen-age chapters with hikes and backpacking planned just for them. Ask for teen-age trips when you write to:

The National Campers and Hikers Association, 7172 Transit Road, Buffalo, NY 14221

The New England Trail Conference, 629 Florence Road, Northampton, MA 01060

Sierra Club, 1050 Mills Tower, 220 Bush Street, San Francisco CA 94104

Backpacking. At the following addresses you will learn about short and long trips for family and teen-age backpacking groups:

Sierra Club, 1050 Mills Tower, 220 Bush Street, San Francisco, CA 94104. Ask for the trips planned in in the U.S. region that interests you.

The Wilderness Society, Western Regional Office, 4260 East Evans Avenue, Denver, CO 80222. July and August trips in all the national forests and parks.

For more information, send 25 cents for *Backpacking in the National Forest Wilderness, a Family Adventure* to Superintendent of Documents, U.S. GPO, Washington, DC 20402

Bicycling. The American Youth Hostel Association is the only address you need if you are interested in maps, tours, hostels, hosteling with groups on a tour, or for touring alone. You must be 14 years old to tour in America and 16 years old to tour abroad. Write to American Youth Hostel Trips, 132 Spring Street, New York, NY 10012.

WILDERNESS AND ADVENTURE CHOICES

Survival Schools. If you are 16½ years old, write to: Outward Bound, Issac Newton Square, Reston, VA 22070, for a list of their survival programs. Wilderness and survival camps are not as easy to find for girls as they are for boys, but here are three that will give you a beginning for a survival school experience.

Rainbow Camp and Wilderness Survival School, Deerlodge National Forest, Box 413, Anaconda, MT 59711 (80 boys and girls from 12 to 18).

North American Wilderness Survival School in the Adirondack Mountains of New York, write to: 205 Lorraine Avenue, Upper Montclair, NJ 07043 (men and women from 15 to 22 years).

Redington Pond School, Wilderness Expedition and Camp, Box 567, Rangeley, ME 04970 (coed from 14 to 19 years).

Mountain Climbing. The three choices listed include instruction in mountain climbing as well as a major climb as part of the experience:

Yosemite Mountaineering, Yosemite National Park, CA 95389 (Alpencraft Seminar—5 day instruction to learn to climb).

The Alpine Club of Canada, General Mountaineering Camp, P.O. Box 1026, Banff, Alberta, Canada (two-week camp for ages over 16).

Canadian Mountain Holidays, 132 Banff Avenue, Box 1660, Banff, Alberta, Canada (The Young Explorer's Camp for ages 12 to 17, one-week sessions; the only camp especially for teens).

Canoeing. Canoe trips are scarce for girls. Try: Camp Darrow, 780 Millbrook Lane, Haverford, PA 19041. And in Canada, a camp especially for girls has canoe trips from 50 to 150 miles and a special eight-week canoe trip for senior canoers on James Bay, directly North of Buffalo, NY. The camp is for ages 13 to 20. Write: Lorien Wilderness Camp, R.D. 1, Wescosville, PA 18106. If you want to join others or organize a family canoe trip, write: Sierra Club for Canoe Trips, 1050 Mills Tower, San Francisco, CA 94104.

River Rafting. Most of the river rafting trips are in the West and are not organized for teen-agers although some teens do go on these trips. Write for details about their hundreds of planned tours for the summer.

American River Touring Association, 1016 Jackson Street, Oakland, CA 94607.

American Guides Association Wilderness Expedition, Woodland, CA 95695.

The Sierra Club for River Rafting, 1050 Mills Tower, San Francisco, CA 94104.

Horseback Riding and Packtripping. Horseback riding trips are mostly in the West, usually for families, but some are planned especially for teen-agers. Write to the following places for a list of their trips in the wilderness:

The Wilderness Society, Western Regional Office, 5850 East Jewel Avenue, Denver, CO 80222.
American Guides Association, Woodland, CA 95495.
The Sierra Club for Packtripping, 1050 Mills Tower, San Francisco, CA 94104.

TRAVEL CHOICES

United States, Canada, and Mexico. Organized groups of teen-agers travel in hotel tours or camping tours as well as cross-country tours by bicycle. Camping, bus, hosteling, and sightseeing tours planned especially for teens:

American Youth Hostels, 20 West 17th Street, New York, NY 10011
Student International Travel Association (SITA), 50 Rockefeller Plaza, New York NY 10020 (tours for 12 years old and over).
Girl Scouts of America, 830 Third Avenue, New York, NY 10022 (several camping travel trips every summer).
Canadian Youth Hostel Association, 86 Scullard Street, Toronto 5, Ontario, Canada.
Arista World Travel, 1 Rockefeller Plaza, New York, NY 10020 (hotel tours for teens).
Fugazy International Travel, 342 Madison Avenue, New York, NY 10017 (teen-agers' hotel tours to Mexico and the West including camping tours of the national parks).
See also Hiking and Biking Choices, Wilderness and Adventure Choices.

Foreign Travel. To get abroad you may live with a foreign family, go to a work camp, study abroad, hostel with an American group, or take regular sightseeing tours. Some possibilities:

Council on International Education Exchange, 777
United Nations Plaza, New York, NY 10017 (ar-
ranges low-cost student travel for individuals or
groups).

American Youth Hostels, 14 West Eighth Street, New
York, NY 10011 (inexpensive bicycle tours; you
must be 16 years old).

Experiment in International Living: 16 to 18 years old,
travel with a group and live with a foreign family
for a month. Very popular program—apply early.
An intensive language training program in Vermont
is included. Write to: High School Programs Abroad,
The Experiment, Putney, VT 05346.

Girl Scouts of the U.S.A. offer many international living
experiences to Senior Scouts. Apply to your local
leader for information.

Israeli Summer Institute: Co-sponsored by the B'nai
B'rith Youth Organization and the Jewish Agency.
Girls aged 15–18 write: B'nai B'rith Youth Organization, 1640 Rhode Island Avenue, N.W., Washington, DC 20036.

The Jewish Agency, Department of Education and Culture, 515 Park Avenue, New York, NY 10022
(several tours to Israel especially for high school
students).

See also Study and Work Camps in this chapter.

STUDY CHOICES

U.S. Study. Check first with your high school teachers
and with the guidance office for study programs at
local high schools, in local centers, in Community Colleges, on college campuses as well as correspondence
schools and camps. Next check School Directories in
the *New York Times,* and in *Redbook, Seventeen,
Parents' Magazine* for summer schools. About 6,000
high school students participate in a National Science
summer study program, ask your science teacher for
appropriate programs for you. See also Art Choices

in this chapter, and the chapter on Learning by Correspondence.

Foreign Study. The two largest private organizations for high school students' foreign study programs are:
American Institute for Foreign Study, 102 Greenwich
    Avenue, Greenwich, CT 06830 (about $1,000 for
    a month at a university center and one week in
    London and Paris, live with family).
Foreign Study League Schools, Pleasantville, New York
    10570. (American teachers and orientation, dormi-
    tories with American chaperons, about $1,000).
See also Foreign Travel and chapter on A Foreign Experience.

ART CHOICES

Art choices for teens can be found at camps, art centers, college campuses, private schools, museums, summer theaters, and in community programs. Check with your high school teachers of art, music, and theater arts, and with the guidance office for local opportunities in the arts. Look at the summer directories in national magazines, for special camps for the arts. The two largest art centers and one campus offer music, art, dance, theater, creative writing and film making.

Chautauqua Summer School, Chautauqua, New York.
    An arts program includes a school of music, dance,
    art and theater for 1,400 high school students. It has
    a special spiritual emphasis including 16 Protestant
    denominational houses that offer Bible study and
    devotional services.
The Banff Centre School of Fine Arts, Banff, Alberta,
    Canada. 1,200 adults, college and high school stu-
    dents meet for the arts above plus ceramics, French,
    voice and opera, radio and TV production.
High School Fine Arts Camp, Arizona State University,
    Temple, AZ 85281.
For music opportunities, look in your local library for

the March 1973 issue of *The Instrumentalist,* a magazine that lists hundreds of summer music programs for teen-agers from rock to opera.

VOLUNTEER AND COMMUNITY SERVICE CHOICES

The first place to look for volunteer work is in your local church/synagogue, school, library, hospital, mental health clinic, or museum. Many of these institutions have established voluntary programs for teenagers and others may find a project for interested students. There are two excellent lists of national volunteer services; send for:

Invest Yourself, an annual pamphlet listing opportunities for voluntary service in the United States and abroad. Send 50 cents to The Commission on Voluntary Service and Action, 475 Riverside Drive, Room 665, New York, NY 10027.

Everyone Can Help Someone as a Volunteer, a booklet with 100 separate volunteer services. Write to National Center for Voluntary Action, 1735 Eye Street, N.W., Washington, DC 20006.

The following agencies have teen-age volunteer programs:

National Center for Voluntary Action, a government agency, 1735 Eye Street, N.W., Washington, DC 20006.

Ecology and Conservation Projects:
The Conservation Foundation, 1717 Massachusetts Avenue, N.W., Washington, DC 20036
Environmental Action, 1346 Connecticut Avenue, Room 731, N.W., Washington, DC 20036
Friends of the Earth, 529 Commercial Street, San Francisco, CA 94111
Bureau of State Parks, Harrisburg, PA 17120 (in

connection with National Campers and Hikers Association).

The Nature Conservancy, 1800 North Kent Street, Arlington, VA 22209.

The Red Cross. Check the Red Cross office nearest you for programs in public relations, fund raising, blood collecting, water safety and disaster preparedness.

Social Action Programs:

American Freedom for Hunger Foundation, 1717 H Street, N.W., Washington, DC 20006

Adventure in Concern, 3802 Houston Street, San Diego, CA 92101

The High School Project of the Robert F. Kennedy Memorial, 3130 M Street, N.W., Washington, DC 20007.

National Park Service, a government project that uses 3,500 teen-age volunteers in the national parks each summer. Write: Office of Information, National Park Service, U.S. Department of Interior, Washington, DC 20240.

See also Work Camps.

JOB CHOICES

Most states require 14-to-16-year-olds to have a work permit or employment certificate verifying their age. This is almost always issued by your local school. Check with your guidance counselor, who will issue your permit, or know where you should get it for the particular state where you want to work.

If you are not yet 16 years old, your best bet for paid jobs will be jobs with young children, jobs around homes and with pets, maintenance work at summer camps, and some national park jobs which are open to 15-year-olds.

If you are 16 years old, you can add to the list counselor or counselor-in-training at summer camps, national parks, ranches, resorts, hotels, restaurants, federal government jobs, and jobs in business and industry.

Look around home, ask your parents and their friends and your neighbors about possible jobs, use the local classified ads in the local and regional newspapers. Here are other ideas:

Jobs with Young Children

Baby sitting

Organize a baby-sitting service

Mother's helper

Tutoring

Planning and organizing children's parties (birthday and holiday)

Bible school or religious summer school teaching

Home and Pets

House watching (water lawns and house plants, check doors and windows daily for owners who are on vacation)

Home services (sweeping, lawn mowing, car washing, shopping)

Painting (inside and out)

Dog walking

Pet sitting (feed, walk, check animals while owners are away)

Boarding pets

Summer Camps

Working in kitchen and laundry for under 16 years

Counselor-in-training for 15- and 16-year-olds

Counselor jobs for 16-to-18-years-olds

Day camp, recreation, and church camp counselor

Information about boarding camp jobs is available at:

Camp Fire Girls, 1740 Broadway, New York, NY 10019

Girl Scouts of USA, Recruitment and Referral Division, 830 Third Avenue, New York, NY 10022

YWCA Projects Director, National Student YWCA, 600 Lexington Avenue, New York, NY 10022

American Camping Association, 342 Madison Avenue, New York, NY 10017

Association of Private Camps, 55 West 42nd Street, New York, NY 10036

National Parks

There are two types of jobs for high school students in U.S. national parks. About 3,000 students from 15 to 18 years old work for the Youth Conservation Corps (YCC). The work includes building trails, planting trees and general ecological work. It is a government job and you can inquire and apply for a list of all the US Youth Conservation Corps projects by writing: YCC, US Department of the Interior, Washington, DC 20204. Then write directly to the national park for a job. Get your application in by January 1, since these jobs are very competitive.

The second type of job in the national parks is with private companies who run the park hotels, lodges, and stores. For a list of these private agencies, write to: National Park Service, U.S. Department of Interior, Washington, DC 20240.

Resort, Hotel, and Restaurant

Jobs in this field include busgirl, dishwasher, salad maker, hamburger clerk, tray-line worker, fountain clerk, pantry worker, hostess, waitress, kitchen helper, short-order cook, sandwich maker, carhop, cook's helper, and cashier. Look in the classified ads, and in the travel and resort sections of the Sunday papers for places to apply for a job. Again, apply early. January and February are the months when resorts hire summer help, and the earlier applications have the best selection of jobs.

Summer Theater and Fine Arts

High school students have the best chance for a job locally. Ask your high school drama, art, music, or English teacher for job ideas in summer theater or the arts. If there is a college or university near you, check with their theater arts, music, and art departments for possible summer jobs.

Government Jobs

There are some jobs in the federal government for the 17-year-old, and many state government jobs are available for 16- and 17-year-olds. The Postal Service hires students in the summer and for Christmas holidays. Check at your local post office for vacancies. Some special programs are created for summer jobs for students—write to your State Personnel Office and ask about their summer jobs for teens. The Highway Department usually hires extra students in the summer to work on construction of new roads, and they are just beginning to hire girls.

Business and Industry

Summer help to replace regular workers on vacation is hired by local banks, stores, business offices; and there are typing jobs, mailroom work, stuffing envelopes, bank teller trainees, messengers, and selling jobs.

If you are interested in a direct selling job, write for a list of businesses that will hire summer high school students to sell their products: Direct Selling Association, 1730 N Street, N.W., Washington, DC 20036.

Whether you are applying in person or writing a letter about your qualifications for a job, the facts employers are most interested in are:

Your training and work experience

Your willingness to work

Your maturity and responsibility—regardless of your age

Your age—if you meet the minimum requirement for the job

The dates you have available for work

Good references about your character

Overseas Summer Jobs

Three agencies are listed for placing English-speaking teen agers in overseas *au pair* jobs. An *au pair* job is taking care of young children in a European family and speaking English to all members of the family. You don't need to know the foreign language, as the family usually knows some English. In some situations, teenagers are exchanged within a family; the students each pay their own transportation.

Ayuda a la Extranjera, Desengaño 9, Madrid 13, Spain. An agency that places American girls with Spanish families for a minimum of 3 months.

The Educational Interchange Council, 43 Russell SW, London, WC1 B 5 DG, England. A home-to-home exchange for 14-to-19-year-olds in France, Germany, Poland, and Switzerland.

Trainees Exchange Office, Siltasaarenkatu 3 A, Helsinki 53, Finland. A government office program. An English-speaking student lives with a Finnish family, teaches English, helps with the housework, receives pocket money from the family. For young women 16 years old who can work from 1 to 3 months.

Making Career Decisions

JOYCE SLAYTON MITCHELL

When children are asked what they are going to be when they grow up, little girls answer, "married"; little boys answer, "a cowboy, a fireman, an astronaut, or a something." All through school boys are expected to work toward the "something" they are going to be; girls are expected to say they are going to be something, but everybody knows that if all goes well, they will be happily married and never use their education. This "marriage only" concept keeps you from making serious good career decisions because it assumes that even if you do work after you are married, you will adapt your job or career to your husband's needs.

No one talks about it—you don't either—but if somewhere in your head is the idea that only what is best for the husband is best for the family, you don't even have a choice in your career decisions. If you still think that the only satisfactory life style available to you is one of a traditional wife and mother there is no way for you freely to choose a career.

There is only one way for you to be married and free for career decisions and that is for you to be planning an equal-partnership marriage. An equal-partnership marriage assumes that whatever the job—child rearing, earning money, or domestic work—it has to be done

*by someone. The "someone" should be decided on the
basis of time available, competency, and interest rather
than race, age, or sex.*

*The world assumes that young men can live where
they want, that their domestic work will be done for
them, and that they can decide how much time, energy,
and space they need to move and grow with a career.
The world assumes that young women's careers will be
their second job (their first being domestic work for
their husband and family) and that their time, energy,
and space will be decided by someone else.*

*If you know now, while you are a student, that you
have the possibility to choose later to get married and
to take a loan for graduate school, to take a field trip
to Australia for research and to have children, to move
from the East to the West for a promotion and to raise
children, and that if you marry, your husband has the
same possibilities—then you are free now to choose
your subjects in school, college, and career. Remember,
lots of men love money-making women! And children
love two parents who share in their upbringing. Mature
adults do love spouse and work and children.*

Careers ARE *for you to plan, and you can plan the
career that is best for you. What is best for each member of a family is the only loving environment possible
for survival.*

What will your life be like five years from now? Ten
years or fifteen years from now? Will you be married?
Will you have children? Will you be working?

If you are like most high school women, you will be
doing all these things at some time in your life. In the
next twenty years you will establish the size of your
family, where you will live, and the type of work you
will do. You can drift into decisions as you go along,
or all these choices can be well thought out. You
would do well to spend some serious thought on the
things you can do most about in your life right now,

namely, your education and selecting your life's work. Plan with care; it's *your* life we are talking about, and you now have a life expectancy of seventy-eight years!

Many young women think ahead to what they can do for a year after college; they think of ways to fill in the time between college and marriage. But most don't look at their work in terms of a career. Careers, they think, are for men, or for women who won't get married, or for a few "ambitious" women. Young men choose a career and start it as soon as they complete school; they never stop working until they retire. This is how a career has been described: uninterrupted, full-time work. Because the career development for young women is different, it is often neglected altogether. The fact is that even though homemaking, child rearing, and community responsibilities cut into a woman's time for paid work, she still has a career pattern. A career pattern for women often consists of working full-time until she has children, no paid work while the children are young, part-time work while the children are in school, and full-time·work again after the children have left home. Even though this is a different pattern than that of men, it is as important to the young woman and to society as full-time paid work.

The world of work for women is a pioneer world in many ways. Because of new civil rights laws giving women equality in promotion and pay opportunities and because educated people are needed in today's society, choices for women are beginning to be broadened and to include some of the same opportunities given to educated men. Never before have the professions, businesses, and government allowed advancement in administrative and executive levels to women. Never before have graduate schools been willing to admit and give scholarships to women. They must now.

Some career information states that women are discriminated against in pay and advancement opportunities. Such statements don't mean that you should give up your idea of going into these careers; but it does mean you should be aware of discrimination, of any lack of equal opportunities. Even though the law now gives women equal rights, our tradition of inequality will for many careers take much longer than a change in laws to overcome. You may be the one to break the tradition and make a few changes toward equal career opportunities for women.

You should know that today most educated women have careers outside their homes. You should know that the largest number of women working in America today are married women 35–45 years of age, with children. By 1980 almost half the work force in the United States will be women, and 90% of all women graduate students will have some contact with paid work. You see the high probability that you will be in this working group.

Your opportunities for finding the right type of work for you—whether it is two days a week, three days a week, no work for five years, or full-time employment —will be increased many times by planning. If you decide to stay home until all your children are out of high school (most women don't), you will be about forty years old and still have twenty-five years of work ahead. Twenty-five years is worth planning for! Plan your education now with a career in mind. A career for you—one that has many variables but allows for marriage and allows for the family responsibilities that couples must assume in marriage.

Helping you to plan for a career while you are going to school and can do something about it is one goal of this book. How does a girl go about choosing a career? After all, you don't yet know the answers to where you will live, what the work opportunities will be, whether you will marry, what your husband will be doing, what your income will be, whether you will have children or how many children you will want to have!

Let's look at what you do know. You know whether you are going to college or not. You know that even though historically a woman's career pattern has been different from a man's career, you can still have a career. You know your school record.

Your past record is always the best place to start when you want to make decisions for where you are headed. After all, school is your occupation, your present career. As you consider what you know about yourself, take an inventory of your school record. Include your grades, your extracurricular activities, your ability to get along with other students, your leadership qualities, your persistence on class projects, your ability to get along with authority. Include your interest in homework and learning.

Using all the information you have about yourself, you can begin to think about your career and how you want to spend your life. The particular subjects you like and do well in can be a beginning for thinking about an occupation. Strong mathematics and physical science background can take you into any one of the many careers in medicine, the physical sciences, or business. Strong English, language, and verbal abilities can take you into publishing or law; and fine arts abilities can take you into museum jobs, or art or writing careers. Remember, too, that many occupations require a well-educated college graduate, regardless of her major. Personnel in these occupations are looking for an alert, responsible, clear-thinking person who can be taught the specifics that are needed for the job.

Your evaluation of yourself through your academic work and extracurricular activites will give you a much clearer idea of your abilities and interests than any test devised to judge you. Remember, this is your performance, not your potential; and this is what counts by the time you are sixteen, seventeen, and twenty-one. Without achievement, all the potential in the world is not apt to change at this point. If you haven't studied as much as you intended to in the last four years, chances are that you won't in the next four years. However, most young women *do* study and make the most of what they have. They usually achieve much more in high school than young men do. One good indication of this is the class rank of the senior class. If you look at the top ten students in a class, you will see the majority are almost always young women, regardless of the test score or potential of the top ten students. This habit of consistent, effective, and responsible work that college-bound women cultivate is a habit that should be continued in college and should lead to a successful career.

Evaluating your needs and values is a little more difficult. Some basic questions may help you to think about them: Do you like to be with people? To work with a team or others your age? To work alone? With children? With the handicapped? Do you like to work with ideas, or things, or towards an ideal? Do you like to be in a complex situation and under pressure of deadlines, or in simple situations, planning each step ahead? A few valuable questions that will influence your career and the types of jobs you choose will include: Do you prefer a particular situation or location, types of people with whom you will not work? Is money the main goal? Do you think you should stay at home if you have preschool children? Will your child-raising responsibilities be shared by your husband? Do you think you would like a job that's short on money but long on prestige? Would you like a job where you can be left to work on your own?

The more you think about your needs and values, the more information you will have for making your life decisions good decisions. After your self-inventory you are ready to start relating this information about yourself to the hundreds of jobs available to you. The first step is to read about the various careers with *you* in mind. Your accomplishments in school, your ambitions, your hopes, and a view toward the specialty of being a woman in a career that may mean interruptions, part-time employment, and often little control over where you live. As you read about different occupations and one sounds just right, write for more information, begin to look around for women and men in the same career to whom you can talk. Make an appointment with them and carefully plan your questions in order to use the time with busy people most effectively.

Read as much as you can about the careers that interest you. *I Can Be Anything: Careers and Colleges for Young Women,* is a book about careers written especially for high school and college women. Remember that all the career information you get must always be related to *you* and your understanding of yourself. When friends tell you the thing for a girl to do is to become a teacher because the vacations are long and the days are short, it won't do you any good if you can't stand to be around groups of children all day long! There is no such thing as one great career for all people, any more than there is one right college, or one right friend, for everyone.

Once you get an idea that makes sense for you, use your summer vacation time for a trial of your idea. Work in a hospital if you are interested in a medical career, with a children's group or in a camp if you are interested in education, in a handicapped camp for children if special education interests you. Try a summer job in a bank or real estate office if business is your interest. There are many summer job possibilities, and using this time to explore career interests pays off better than waiting on tables even though you may earn more money as a waitress.

There are some things educators know about vocational development for students which may be helpful to you as you work on your career development. First, choosing a career is a long process rather than a choice out of the blue. You are selecting your career possibilities as you select your curriculum in high school and college, when you take French IV in place of Mathematics IV. You made one of your biggest selections in career possibilities when you elected Algebra I in place of General Mathematics back in the eighth grade. As you choose your college and your college major, you are making career choices.

Second, there is no one occupation which is the right one for all women. People have many career potentialities, usually related, where they can use all they have to offer and find satisfaction in their work. Third, most everyone compromises in their final career outcome. This is especially true for women, who usually go along with the many family circumstances in their lives because they so often go where their husbands go. And last, career changes are costly and time-consuming. For instance, women who have majored in English literature in college, then ten years later decide to teach, must go back to school and fulfill the necessary requirements for teaching. If more planning during college had been done with a better realization of women's career patterns, much of this extra effort at a later date could have been avoided. Again, plan while you are in school to increase your chance of finding work opportunities no matter where you live at a later time in your life.

In planning your college selection consider the numbers and percentages of women in particular majors. The college with the most number of women in your major may not be the college most suited to you, but the number of women in the program is a factor you should consider when selecting your college. Both the number of women and the ratio of men to women should be considered. The other considerations of admission—cost, programs offered, test requirements, type of campus life, locations and scholarship opportunities—can be found in the chapter "Choosing Your College."

Career experts say that the people who are happiest in their work are the ones who get a chance to use everything they are and have an opportunity to handle as much responsibility as they are capable of handling. The main idea for you is to look at who you are and decide who you can become. The age-old story that a young woman has to have something to do in case something happens to her husband or in case she doesn't get married is not a satisfactory way of choosing a career. You will want to choose a career because you are a bright, talented young woman who has something to offer this world in terms of your abilities, your time, and your values. Wanting to marry and raise a family does not in any way cut you out from the responsibility of decision making about a career while you are in school.

There are hundreds of jobs in many career lines—any one of which a woman can do. In order to give you an idea of the range of possibilities beyond the usual teaching, nursing, and secretarial possibilities prescribed for all women, a list of careers follows. Most of the careers in the list require a minimum of two years of college or higher education.

America today offers women more options for working than at any other time in history. You have more chances than women have ever had to decide what careers are best for you, what years are best for you, and how you want work to fit into your life style.

CAREERS FOR THE COLLEGE-BOUND

Accountant
Actress
Actuary
Advertising Careers
Airline Pilot and
    Flight Engineer
Anthropologist
Archaeologist
Architect
Army
Artist
Astronomer
Athlete
Automobile Dealer
    and Sales
Banking Careers
Biologist

Book Publishing Careers
Botanist
Business Executive
Chemist
Chiropractor
Choreographer
City Planner
Civil Service Careers
Clergy
College Professor
College Student
    Personnel Careers
Commercial Artist
Computer Programmer
Conservation Careers
Copywriter
Dancer

Data Processor
Dean of Students
Dental Hygienist
Dentist
Designer
Dietitian
Doctor
Early Childhood
  Educator
Earth Science Careers
Ecologist
Economist
Editor
Education Administrator
Elementary School
  Teacher
Engineer
Fashion Careers
Federal Bureau of
  Investigation Careers
Flight Attendant
Foreign Language Careers
Foreign Service Careers
Forester
Funeral Director
Geographer
Geologist
Geophysicist
Group Work
Guidance Counselor
High School Teacher
Historian
Home Economist
Hospital Administrator
Hotel-Motel Careers
Industrial Designer
Insurance Business
  Careers
Interior Designer
  and Decorator

Interpreter
Journalist
Lawyer
Librarian
Magazine Publishing
  Careers
Market Research Careers
Mathematician
Medical Assistant
Medical Record
  Librarian
Medical Technologist
Mental Health Careers
Merchandising
Meteorologist
Military Careers
Minister
Missionary
Museum Careers
Music Careers
Navy
Newspaper Publishing
  Careers
Nurse
Nursery School Teacher
Occupational Therapist
Oceanographer
Optometrist
Peace Corps
Personnel Careers
Pharmacist
Photographer
Physical Education
  Teacher
Physical Therapist
Police Officer
Political Scientist
Priest
Psychiatrist
Psychologist

Public Relations Careers
Radio and Television
  Careers
Real Estate Careers
Recreation Careers
Rehabilitation Counselor
Religious Careers
Secretary
Social Worker
Sociologist
Special Education
  Teacher

Speech and Hearing
  Therapist
Statistician
Stock Broker
Surgical Technician
Technical Writer
Travel Agent
United Nations Careers
Veterinarian
Writing Careers
Youth Service Careers
Zoologist

Choosing a Trade, Technical, or Business Career

KENNETH B. HOYT

Ken Hoyt is the associate commissioner in the U.S. Office of Education. As Director of Career Education, he is establishing career education programs for special groups of students to include women. Dr. Hoyt tells us that our taxes are rapidly expanding the vocational-technical-occupational training programs because these skills are needed in the work force, and that 90 percent of today's high school women will spend some time working. Yet almost no women are taking advantage of vocational training other than in traditional areas of health, secretarial, and cosmetology.

Broaden your view of what you can do and what you choose to do in vocational training. It isn't just for women who can't go to college; it's for everyone who has an interest in a trade, technical, or business career.

What will you do if you don't go to college? Educators often assume that you are either not going to work at all or will take unskilled jobs that require little or no specialized training. This flies in the face of the currently rapidly expanding call for persons equipped with specialized occupational skills heard throughout the occupational world today. The U.S. Department of Labor has estimated that, of the jobs that will exist between now and 1980, fewer than 20 percent will require a college diploma. At the same time, opportunities that require no specific occupational skills are declining. Between the unskilled laborer and the college graduate, there exists a very wide variety of technical, skilled occupations requiring vocational training.

Many people seem to feel that if you want vocational training you can find all the opportunities you need in the health occupations, in the secretarial field, and in the area of cosmetology. While each of these fields is undergoing rapid expansion, there is absolutely no reason for you to limit yourself to such specific fields in considering possible career choices.

Vocational training is one possible career choice for you. You should know just as clearly and as forcefully as it can be said that this is: (1) a rapidly growing area; (2) an area in which young women can complete training successfully; and (3) an area in which occupational opportunities for women are opening up rapidly.

VOCATIONAL EDUCATION

High school vocational education offerings are found in both comprehensive high schools and in area vocational schools that students attend on a half-day basis with the other half-day spent in their "home" high school. At this level, basic vocational skill training is offered in an increasingly large number of areas—including health, agribusiness, business and office occupations, food services, personal services, consumer and homemaking education, marketing and distribution, and trade and industrial occupations. If you have such a set of offerings in your high school, we would urge you to visit the shops, laboratories, and training areas. Look at the equipment. Talk to current students and instructors. Try to keep asking yourself the question, "What is being taught here that I could not learn?" If you do, you should very quickly come up with the answer, *"I can learn the skills taught in every area of vocational education."*

Yet, if you examine enrollments in such programs, you will find most young women enrolled in the home-making, business and office occupations, marketing, food services, and personal service areas. We still have mostly young men enrolled in courses such as auto mechanics, machinist, electronics, or welding. There are, of course, a growing number of exceptions. For example, a young woman took third place in the national welding contest conducted by the Vocational Industrial Clubs of America in 1973. The question remains, what is being taught in vocational education courses that you could not learn? The answer remains, nothing. The days when extremely high degrees of physical strength were required for occupational success have disappeared in every occupational area taught in high school vocational education programs. Yet, this has not been reflected with an increasing number of young women enrolled in what have been traditionally male-dominated courses.

The same trends are also seen at the post-high school level, both in our community colleges and in the private trade, technical, and business schools throughout the country. It is at the post-high school level where the highest degrees of vocational skill are offered. This vocational training prepares people to perform successfully as skilled craftsworkers and technicians in the current occupational world. We have seen the community college movement mushroom in the United States with over 1,200 currently existing and almost one new community college opening somewhere in the country on the average of once a week. Yet, young women who enroll in such community colleges are typically not taking advantage of advanced vocational training offered in such fields as electronics, drafting, computer technology, environmental technology, household repair, watch and jewelry repair, or police science—to mention just a few. Think about such fields for a minute. Is there any reason to believe that you could not succeed in any of those fields? Of course there isn't!

Similar observations can be made when we look at students at the almost 8,500 private trade, technical, and business schools offering post-high school occupational education programs throughout the United States. We find private business school secretarial courses filled primarily with women, but accounting courses filled primarily with men. Most of the cosmetology and fashion design students are women (although increasing numbers of men are entering both fields). However, when we look at enrollments in private vocational schools training people to be truck drivers, heavy earth-moving equipment operators, welders, diesel mechanics, electronic technicians, or computer programmers, we find very few women enrolled. Again, if one asks, "Why," the answer obviously is not that the training requires skills, or abilities or physical strength that women do not possess. Instead, it only reflects the kinds of occupational biases that still exist in our culture that regard such occupations as ones "for men only."

In short, growing numbers of vocational training programs in a wide variety of vocational-technical-occupational areas are being established throughout the United States at both the high school and post-high school levels. Hundreds of millions of tax dollars are being spent in the construction and operation of such training opportunities. In the case of those supported by public funds, it is obvious that they should be available to the *public*—and the "public" includes you!

WHY HAVEN'T WOMEN ENROLLED?

Primarily, tradition has prevented women from taking advantage of the current rapid expansion of occu-

pational education. The "excuses" used for excluding
and/or discouraging women from enrolling in such
courses are easily spelled out and include: (1) the
work is too hard for women to perform; (2) women
don't like to get their hands dirty; (3) the language
used in the workplace would be offensive to women;
(4) employers wouldn't hire women if they were
trained in such occupations; and (5) occupational hazards, in terms of danger or accident, are too great to
justify women entering such occupations. Such excuses
are purely and simply inexcusable in these times. Every
excuse is contrary to the facts. All trends currently
available in hiring and work practices point to the
increasing falsehood of these excuses.

There is only *one* really good reason why women
do not elect a field of occupational education. That
reason is that some may not *choose* to do so. The
problem we face at the present time is that women are
not being given the opportunity to choose occupational
education. Instead, they are being systematically ex-
cluded (or at least actively discouraged) from entering
such training. With the current great national effort
being exerted to expand and improve vocational education at all levels in a wider and wider variety of
areas, it is simply time that the choices being created
by such expansion be fully as available to you as they
currently are to young men. If, given such conditions,
you *choose* something else, that is one thing. To deny
you as great a variety of choices as young men is quite
another.

HOW DO YOU KNOW IF YOU
WANT A VOCATIONAL CAREER?

People who succeed in vocational careers are ones
who have learned that education of the hands and the
mind go together. Today many people still believe that
they should choose between "working with their head"

or "working with their hands," as though to do either precluded the other. The most important thing to understand, for any person considering a vocational career today, is that you have to be the kind of person who has interest in both "thinking" and "doing."

A trade, technical, or business career may be just what you are looking for. Are you the kind of person who:

> Has interest in *both* thinking and doing?
>
> Really wants to learn things that will help you get a job?
>
> Is willing to work hard in order to get a set of job skills?
>
> Doesn't like to study unless there's a direct tie-in with the kind of work you hope to do when you finish?
>
> Has a good idea of the kind of work you would like to do?
>
> Likes to learn things that help you *do* something concrete and productive on your job after learning?

If so, a vocational career rather than four years in college may be the best thing you could do to prepare for work.

Thousands of private trade, technical, and business schools exist throughout the United States. The community college is opening its doors to students who want trade, technical or business training. Hundreds of public area vocational schools operating at the post-high school level now exist in this country. Each of these represents a possible training opportunity for you. Should you choose one? If so, which one? Choosing a vocational school wisely requires a lot of thought on your part—and a lot of information. Here are some questions we have found thousands of students asking as they thought about going into a vocational career. Maybe you have some of the same questions. Hopefully, by studying these questions, you may discover for yourself a better basis for making your decisions.

What kinds of students would I be competing against if I went to this school?

How long would it take me to finish my training?

How much is the tuition? What would my *total* costs be?

How do students here pay the costs?

What kind of housing would I find?

Do students find part-time jobs while in school? If so, how much do they work? How much do they earn?

How much do students study?

How do students judge the school's equipment? Its instructors? How do they rate the school in general? Does it come up to the expectations students held for it?

What percentage of students going to that school actually finish their training? How many drop-out?

What kinds of jobs do students get after training here? Do they get full-time jobs? Are those jobs directly related to the training they received?

Where do students find jobs after completing training? How much money do they earn on those jobs? How well do they like the jobs they found after training? How fast do they get promoted or get a raise?

In the long run, the key question you need to answer for yourself is, WHAT IS LIKELY TO HAPPEN TO ME IF I GO TO THAT SCHOOL AND TAKE THAT TRAINING? By trying to find specific answers to questions such as listed above, you will be in the best possible position to get some answer to this "jackpot" question.

How will you find answers to questions such as these? Try as many as possible of the following approaches:

Visit the school and look around before deciding to go. There is no good substitute for a personal visit. While there, talk with some of the students in training as well as with school officials. Be sure to ask for a tour of the building(s).

Ask for a school catalogue and all other literature the school has available for prospective students. If you have questions regarding items in the catalogue, ask school officials either in person or in writing.

Study the school's application form carefully. Find out if a down payment is required and, if so, how much you have to pay and what part of it you get back if you don't attend or if you attend for just a short while.

If it is a private trade, technical, or business school, get answers to each of the following questions:

—If it is a private *trade* or *technical* school, ask, "Are you accredited by the National Association of Trade and Technical Schools? If so, when were you accredited?"

—If it is an *engineering technician* school, ask, "Is the specific training program I am considering accredited by the Engineer's Council on Professional Development?"

—If it is a private *business* school, ask, "Is this school accredited by the Accrediting Commission for Business Schools? Is this school a member of the United Business Schools Association?"

No matter what type of private school, ask

—Are students attending this school eligible for loans under the Higher Education Act of 1965?

—Is this school approved for veterans training? For training under the state Division of Vocational Rehabilitation? For training under the Manpower Development and Training Act?

A "No" answer to any of the above questions should cause you to wonder further about whether this is a good school for you.

Try to find as many students as possible who have attended the school. Write—or better yet, visit—with each of them and ask them questions such as listed above. Don't be content with answers given you by only one student. Try to ask you questions of as many students as you can.

Ask the school to give you a list of some employers who have hired their graduates. Write a few such employers and ask for their opinions regarding training the school provides.

Visit with a professional school counselor about your decision. In such visits, remember you are not trying to find out which school is "best" in any general sense. Instead, you are trying to find out which is "best" for *you*.

Visit with some other adult—parents, relatives, or friends about your decision. It will help to talk to many people. It won't hurt if you hear conflicting things. After all, in the end you will make up your own mind.

Above all, don't hurry about making your decision. Take your time. Don't be afraid to ask for more information whenever you want it. Wait until you feel sure this is a good thing for you to do before signing up.

IN CONCLUSION

Trade, technical, and business training at both the secondary and post-secondary level represents one of the fastest growing parts of American education. The training offered in such programs is directly relevant to many of the new and expanding occupations called for in our increasingly technical and complex occupational economy. No current occupational education course requires skills that you can't develop. With *90 percent of today's high school women* predicted to spend some time employed, it is obvious that they ought to take advantage of vocational training. Is a vocational career for you? Only you can answer. The point being made here is that the *opportunity to choose* trade, technical, or business training—or to refuse to choose it—belongs to you.

Choosing Your College

JOYCE SLAYTON MITCHELL

There are many ways to go about selecting a college. One way is to go to the college closest to your home where you know the largest number of students. Another is to drift into the decision at the last minute and go to the college that is recruiting the hardest for students. Many students select a college by a particular program offered, or career decision.

The trend toward making all colleges coeducational shouldn't keep you from considering a woman's college. Even though men/women relationships in an everyday natural atmosphere are good values, for some students an all-women's atmosphere can best prepare you now for male/female relationships later.

A woman has to feel like an equal person before she can have an equal relationship with another person. One way to learn to be who you can be is to separate yourself from men in a woman's college and have a chance to learn without male visibility or competition for a few years. You can learn to be an achiever, a leader in publications, sports, and student government in a way that is often difficult for women in a coeducational college. The sports facilities will be yours at all hours—not just the times the men don't want the pool, or gym, or courts. A woman's college is a place where women are in leadership positions as part of your fa-

culty and administration in numbers such as you have never seen before nor will ever see again.

For those of you who select a coeducational college as the right environment for your growth and learning, remember that these colleges, too, are beginning to deal with feminist issues. Some have special seminars taught by well-know feminists, while many offer women's studies courses and a degree in women's studies.

The crucial question that all of you must consider as you select your college is, "Knowing who I am, what I can do, what my interests are . . . which colleges have the most to do with me, where I can make the most of who I am?" When you get as much information about the college as the college gets about you, then you will have the basis for a good decision.

The place to begin your search for a college is with *you*. It's not the college or the university, but *you*, you need to know most about how to make a good decision about where to go after high school.

Deciding not to worry about getting into college doesn't help. Just when you aren't thinking about it, a magazine or newspaper or TV program comes out with new recruiting programs to get you interested in their college, and there you are, thinking about colleges again.

The first thing you can do about colleges at the beginning of your high school career is to learn what kind of a student you are. If you take the strongest program that you can handle well while in high school, you will learn how it feels to be the kind of a student you are. Some students work very hard and decide they really don't like it and choose a less competitive college or a program that is more practical than academic.

The next thing you can do during your first two years of high school is to listen and read whenever you hear someone talking about a specific college, and go to any programs your school has open to freshman and sophomores for college information. Whenever you hear a college representative recruiting for the college s/he represents, make an effort to notice where the information is coming from. When your aunt tells you there is no place like Central U., remember, it was fifteen years ago that she was there. When a young woman on your street tells you how unfriendly all the students are at Northern U., keep in mind that she didn't have any friends at high school either. So be sure you know who says what, and make an opinion about the source of information as well as the information.

There are many ways to select a college. One way is to go to the college closest to your home where you know the most number of students. Another is to drift into the choice at the last minute and go to the college that is recruiting the hardest for students. Many students select a college by a particular program offered, or because they have decided upon a particular career. Still another way to select a college is to make a systematic survey of all the universities and colleges available and to select a few that have the most meaning for you. When you get as much information about the college as the college gets about you, then you will have the basis for a good decision.

Too many students concentrate their search for a college on the basis of whether they can meet the admission requirements, or where it is located, or its tuition and living fees. These are certainly important factors, but it is also essential to understand in some detail what the college is like and if it is a setting in which you are likely to achieve success. You must ask more than, can I get in? You must also ask, what will it be like after I get in? Only then can you begin to ask yourself, what are the implications for me of one type of college life over another type? Will I be different if I go to a collegiate type college, or an experimental college, or a college for women? What effect will one campus atmosphere have on my selection of friends, of spouse, and on my religious, political, and career values?

A student choosing a college has much the same job as a college admissions officer selecting a student. From your record s/he can look at your height, weight, age, college board scores, and marks; you can look at cost, location, programs offered, and requirements for admission to a college. However, until the admissions officers meets you personally and reviews personality reports from your high school, s/he doesn't have a precise idea of who you really are.

The many college guides on the market today will give you the range of options in higher education by describing each college. You can learn about enrollment, size of community where the college is located, programs offered, cost, level of competition for admission, sororities on campus, and campus life. The two basic and complete guides for you to look at are *The College Handbook* edited by Douglas D. Dillenbeck (College Entrance Examination Board), and *Comparative Guide to American Colleges* by James Cass and Max Birnbaum (Harper & Row). In addition there are several good guides written by college students that you will like and that will give you a student's view of what the college life will be like. The best of these is *The Underground Guide to the College of Your Choice* by Susan Berman (Signet Books). The best source for scholarships and financial aid is published each year and you can order *Meeting Your College Costs* free from the College Entrance Examination Board, Box 592, Princeton, New Jersey 08540. It gives step-by-step directions for when and where to apply for financial aid.

The characteristics you need in a college will be the result of your past school record; your family background; the size of the community in which you grew up; your interests, abilities, and educational and career plans for your future. As you go through the college guides and find categories important to you, note the colleges that occur several times in your choices, and read many descriptions of the college by different sources to try to get a total picture. Some colleges will sound good immediately; they will feel right for you, while others will not. If your selections are limited to one or two colleges, go through your criteria again and be more flexible on some kinds of information in order to get as wide a range as you think would work for you at this time. Undergraduates should look at broad offerings in programs rather than at specifics. If you are interested in physical science, you may end up in some physical science but not necessarily in biology, which may be your main interest right now. If you are like most prospective undergraduates, you aren't quite sure what you want to be, or which program is best for you. If you do choose a program, chances are that you will change programs before you actually graduate. Many courses open to you at college are courses that will be completely new to you.

Reading about college life on a campus will give you an idea of differences among college cultures. When you compare the rules of various colleges, you will learn about their differences regarding student responsibilities and college authority. You will get an idea of campus character or personality. It should be clear that the campus atmosphere does not indicate the degree of academic competition for admission. You cannot tell how hard it is to get into a college by the number of hours the library is open. Conversely, you don't have to be a superior student to find a college with an intellectual atmosphere and where much of the responsibility for her work is given to the student. And the opposite is true. Many colleges that take only above average and superior students have a collegiate rather than intellectual atmosphere, with little academic or social responsibility given to the students.

Whatever the rules of the campus, you must relate them to your expectation of college. Look for the type of campus life you think will be most successful and most productive for you. Find a culture or setting that gives you an opportunity to try out your interests and abilities. Choose a setting that gives you the kind of support and encouragement you need. If you don't have a brother, and have few male friends, you may find that coed living makes you too uptight to cope academically. You must relate your findings about the differences in college life to yourself. Your findings have no meaning for anyone else. You can see that some of your friends would want and need a very different type of setting than you want. Ask yourself, "To what degree can I take academic and social responsibility?" "How much responsibility do I take now for my social life?" "How strict are my parents in their rules in relation to the college rules?" "In what kinds of classroom climate do I work the hardest?" "How do the colleges that I am looking at relate to what I know about myself and the degree of responsibility that I take?"

These questions must be considered seriously as you look at colleges and make your choices, if you want an idea of what a college will be like *before* you get there!

Not often mentioned for your college selection plan is the fact that, after you decide the ideal college for you, you must also make a second, third, and fourth choice. Sometimes you must settle for your third and fourth choice, so make those choices as acceptable to you as your first choice. You often have to learn the meaning of compromise on a public or visible level for the first time. Until this time in your life, your compromises and disappointments didn't have to be known to quite as many people. Your grades may have been a little lower than you had hoped, or you may not have had as good a part in the play as you had in mind. But you didn't make public your expectation as you must with college applications. The college acceptance, rejection, or wait list is seen by friends, teachers, and parents.

The social visibility of your college choice presents many problems to everyone. One of the most complicating factors is that you and your parents may not agree with what group or subgroup you want to be identified. For you, Reed College sounds just right; but your parents feel a liberal campus will hinder their status in the community, and they want you to go to Middlebury. You often waver back and forth between wanting the college you want and wanting your parent's approval; you know you can't have both.

If you are clear about the kind of college you think would be ideal for you, most effective for you, you will have little difficulty making your first choice. The trouble comes when you are looking for your second and third choices *within* your ideal type that have different levels of academic competition for admission. Many students would rather switch their criteria for selecting the college with the best environment and program for them than to violate their self-image and go to a third- or fourth-choice college they never heard of.

For instance, a senior selects Wellesley as her ideal college. The counselor suggests Wheaton (Massachusetts) as a second choice, Wells as a third choice, and William Smith as her last choice. If the student isn't from the East and hasn't heard of Wells or William Smith, she doesn't like telling people that she may go there even though the atmosphere, values of the college, and percentage of liberal arts students going on to graduate school are very similar to her first choice. The one big difference in the four colleges is the academic level of competition for admissions, and for intellectual work. She decides to apply at Boston University and Ohio State, because everyone knows those colleges.

All of a sudden the student has gone from what is best for me to "Where can I get in that looks good to me, and to people I care about?" You are giving all the reasons why a certain type of college and education is best for you and then you completely disregard these reasons in order to find a visibly acceptable college. Your self-image counts. The social visibility of your college choice counts. But you must deal with aspects of your choice and get them together. You must try to see a relationship between you and your college applications.

Select a first right, and a second and third right. Representatives from colleges are a good source of information for you. Don't let them get all the facts as if their purpose of recruitment is more important than you finding out about their college. The college admissions scene has changed drastically to the student's advantage. Ask questions—questions that concern you, not necessarily the college's latest idea of what students want to know. Knowing you as you do, you can't fit into someone else's idea of education for you and spend your high school years in preparation for their concept of education. Look at all the possibilities and ask, "Knowing what I do about me, what colleges are best for me?"

A Foreign Experience:
Study Abroad

JOYCE SLAYTON MITCHELL

This chapter provides you with the information you need to select a foreign university or program on your own. If you want a foreign study experience, it does not have to be selected by your high school or some special program. You can plan your own experience.

To help you to decide where to study, this chapter includes the names and addresses of evaluation studies of high school programs; clearinghouses that place thousands of high school students in summer and thirteenth-year foreign study programs; two educational organizations that help students with foreign travel, study, and planning; guides to study abroad. For more information, it provides names and addresses from specific countries where most Americans enroll for foreign university-level study.

American students have gone from East to West, from West to Midwest to South; they have scattered all over the United States to find the college of their choice. Some students have gone abroad for a year or a semester or a summer or a degree.

There are many reasons for Americans going to international universities for their education. The biggest reason is for the adventure of a foreign experience, of going to another country and living in a culture with friends from a diversity of nations. Even if it's adjoining countries like French Canada or Mexico, the living and learning experience is that of a new culture and a total change in environment, language, food, climate, and people.

There are over 32,000 U.S. students abroad and officially enrolled (matriculated) in a foreign university-level institution. Added to that number are the thousands of American students enrolled in nondegree programs, high school programs, special programs for American students, summer programs, and short-term programs.

INDEPENDENT STUDY

If you want to go to a foreign university, you don't have to wait to be selected in a program sponsored by your high school or college. Many students who would like to spend one or two years in foreign study select their own university or program.

Evaluation Guides especially for high school programs abroad are available if you are planning to go on your own. Write for:

Guidelines for the Appraisal of Travel-Study Tours for Secondary School Students. Commission on Secondary Schools, North Central Association, 4554 South Shore Drive, Chicago, IL 60615. Free.

Study Abroad: Suggestions for Selecting Study-Travel Tours for Secondary Students. U.S. Department of Health, Education and Welfare. GPO, Washington, DC 20402. 15 cents.

Evaluation of U.S. Programs Abroad: A Bibliography. Institute of International Education, 809 United Nations Plaza, New York, NY 10017. Free.

HIGH SCHOOL AND THIRTEENTH-YEAR PROGRAMS

The following four organizations send thousands of high school students abroad for study each year. If you want to plan your way to go, write:

American Year Abroad, 225 East 46th Street, New York, NY 10017. An excellent program for students who want to go to Paris or Madrid and live with a family their first year out of high school.

American Institute for Foreign Study, 102 Greenwich Avenue, Greenwich, CT 06830. A major clearinghouse that sends thousands of high school students to live with a family and study at a foreign university.

Youth for Understanding, 2013 Whashtenaw Avenue, Ann Arbor, MI 48104. Many thirteenth-year Study Abroad programs in all parts of the world; live with a local family.

International Christian Youth Exchange, 55 Liberty Street, New York, NY 10005. Home stay in Europe, Latin America, Asia, New Zealand; for 16-to-19-year-olds.

HIGH SCHOOL SUMMER PROGRAMS OF STUDY

See chapter on "Summer Time Is Discovery Time," Study Choices: Foreign Study.

EDUCATIONAL ORGANIZATIONS FOR AMERICANS ABROAD

The two organizations that follow can provide you with information you need about visas, passports, and exchange programs. They have brochures, pamphlets, books and guides in addition to information about foreign study for Americans in any country in the world. Be specific about where and when you want to go when you write and ask about Study Abroad to:

Institute of International Education, 809 United Nations Plaza, New York, NY 10017.
Council on International Educational Exchange, 777 United Nations Plaza, New York, NY 10017.

GUIDES TO STUDY ABROAD

Look for the following guides in your local library or bookstore or send to the publisher for them. The following are especially good and they include summer and academic programs for high school students.

Whole World Handbook, Council on International Educational Exchange, 777 United Nations Plaza, New York, NY 10017. Latest edition. A complete list of opportunities for student travel, work and study abroad, easy to read, and the best of its kind. $2.95.
The New Guide to Study Abroad, by Garraty, Adams, and Taylor (Harper & Row). 1974–75 edition. A complete guide to foreign study programs. $2.95.
The Guide to Canadian Universities, by Joyce Slayton Mitchell (Simon & Schuster of Canada). 1970. A special section for American students including the admission requirements for Americans for each university. $2.95.

U.S. STUDENTS ABROAD

The following countries are where the largest number of American students are officially enrolled in university-level programs. The students in nonofficial programs raise the number of Americans studying in these countries to the tens of thousands.

1. France 6,072
2. Canada 5,265
3. Mexico 4,109
4. Great Britain 2,416
5. Germany 2,133
6. Italy 1,677
7. Spain 1,654

8. Israel 1,405
9. Philippines 1,021
10. Japan 996
11. South America—
    Colombia 580
12. Oceania/Australia
    202

WHERE TO GET MORE INFORMATION

The countries are arranged in order of the largest number of officially enrolled university-level U.S. students. Most materials listed below are free.

FRANCE

Write to: French Cultural Services
972 5th Avenue, New York, NY 10021

Ask for: 1. *Studies in France.* General Information
2. *Courses for Foreigners in France: Summer*
3. *Courses for Foreigners in France: Academic Year*
4. *Specialized Summer Studies*
5. *Study of Music in France*
6. *Elementary and Secondary School in France*

CANADA

Write to: Canadian Consulate
680 5th Avenue, New York, NY 10019

Ask for: *University Study in Canada*
See: *Guide to Canadian Universities,* in this chapter under Guides to Study Abroad

MEXICO

Write to: Embassy of Mexico
2829 – 16th Street, N.W., Washington, DC 20009

Ask for: Study opportunities for American students in Mexico.

Write to: Institute of International Education, 809 United Nations Plaza, New York, NY 10017

Ask for: Profile on Mexico

GREAT BRITAIN *Write to:* British Information Services 845 Third Avenue, New York, NY 10022

Ask for:
1. Short Courses and Summer Schools in Britain
2. Some Notes for the Guidance of Overseas Students Who Wish to Study at British Universities
3. Art Schools in Britain
4. Drama Schools in Britain
5. Music Schools in Britain
6. Communication Media Schools in Britain

Write to: Central Bureau for Educational Visits and Exchanges, 43 Dorset Street, London W1H 3FN, England

Ask for: Study Opportunities for American students in Great Britain

GERMANY *Write to:* German Consulate 460 Park Avenue, New York, NY 10022

Ask for:
1. Goethe Institute — Language Courses
2. A Directory for Teachers and Students of German

Write to: German Academic Exchange Service, 1 5th Avenue, New York, NY 10003

Ask for: 1. *Academic Studies in the Federal Republic of Germany*

Write to: Institute of International Education, 809 United Nations Plaza, New York, NY 10017

Ask for: *Study in Germany*

ITALY

Write to: Italian Cultural Institute, 686 Park Avenue, New York, NY 10021

Ask for: 1. *Summer Courses in Italy*
2. *Rules for the Admission of Foreign Students to Italian Universities*
3. *Artistic Education*
4. *Academic Programs in Italy Sponsored by American Universities and Colleges*

Write to: Institute of International Education, 809 United Nations Plaza, New York, NY 10017

Ask for: 1. *Study in Italy*
2. *The Study of Art in Italy*
3. *The Study of Music in Italy*

SPAIN

Write to: Consulate General of Spain, Cultural Department, 150 East 58th Street, New York, NY 10022

Ask for: 1. *Study in Spain—Highlights for Americans*
2. *Courses for Foreign Students in Spain*
3. *Information for American Students on the Span-*

*ish Educational System
and Spanish Universities*

Write to: Institute of International
Education, 809 United Na-
tions Plaza, New York, NY
10017

Ask for: 1. *Study in Spain*—a 27-
page profile with lists of
universities and programs

ISRAEL

Write to: Israel Government Tourist
Office, 574 5th Avenue,
New York, NY 10036

Ask for: Study opportunities for
American students in Israel

Write to: Institute of International
Education, 809 United Na-
tions Plaza, New York, NY
10017

Ask for: *Study in the Middle East*—
an 8-page pamphlet with
programs offered in English

PHILIPPINES

Write to: Philippines Consulate
15 East 66 Street, New
York, NY 10021

Ask for: Study opportunities for
American students in the
Philippines

Write to: Institute of International
Education, 809 United Na-
tions Plaza, New York, NY
10017

Ask for: *Study in the Philippines*

Write to: YSTAPHIL Paez Building,
90 South Padre Faura, Er-
mita, Manila, Philippines

Ask for: List of student travel centers

JAPAN

Write to: Association of International
Education Japan, c/o Ko-

maba 4-chrome, Meguro-ku, Tokyo 53, Japan

Ask for: Life and Study in Japan. $1.00

Write to: Institute of International Education, 809 United Nations Plaza, New York, NY 10017

Ask for: Study in Japan

Write to: Association for Asian Studies, 1 Lane Hall, University of Michigan, Ann Arbor, MI 48104

Ask for: Study opportunities for American students in Japan

SOUTH AMERICA *Write to:* Institute of International Education, 809 United Nations Plaza, New York, NY 10017

Ask for: Profiles on Argentina, Caribbean, Chile, Brazil, Central America, Mexico, Colombia, and Peru

Write to: Department of Educational Affairs, General Secretariat, Organization of American States, 17th Street and Constitution Avenue, N.W., Washington, DC 20006

Ask for: List of higher educational institutions in any of the specific South American countries that interest you

AUSTRALIA *Write to:* Australian News and Information Bureau, 636 5th Avenue, New York, NY 10020

Ask for: Facilities for Higher Education in Australia

Write to: Institution of International Education, 809 United Nations Plaza, New York, NY 10017

Ask for: *Study in Australia*—a 21-page booklet

Write to: Council on International Educational Exchange, 777 United Nations Plaza, New York, NY 10017

Ask for: *Student Guide* by Australian Union of Students (a travel guide with discounts for students in Australia; $1.50)

The Women Of America Series from Laurel-Leaf Library

PB 339
15